Veiled Allusions

Vicky Hamilton

White Witch of the West Press

Veiled Allusions

2024 © Vicky Hamilton

ISBN
978-0-9969662-8-3

Cover Design
MIRROR, MIRROR 2002,
Charcoal & Graphite on Paper
27.3"x19.7"
©LaurieLipton

Typeset, Layout and Illustrations
Cayley Credit

Back Cover
Liz Koskenmaki

Vicky's Dress
Matrushka Construction

Painting
Eric Montoya
Entitled: Carpe Diem

"Without this guy I would be totally fucked. Thank you for editing my book. Now I owe you two guitars."

Peter M. Margolis
Editor

Dedication

I would like to dedicate this book to all the people who
follow their dreams, but mostly to those who have
helped me achieve mine!

At the top of that list (in regard to this book) would be:

Holly Browde, Eric Smith, Mark Walbaum,
Cayley Credit, Iris Berry, Peter Margolis,
Laurie Lipton, Mitchell Schneider, Marcee
Rondan, and Pat Egan

Special Thanks
to

Iris Berry, Micheal Holdaway, Caroline McElroy,
Bradley Bello, Debarah Hanan, Susan Macintosh,
Voxx, Pamela Morrison, Bobby Kravitz and Arlene
Drake.

For the endless conversations working on my neurosis.

Foreword

I consider it an extreme honor to be invited to write a foreword. Especially for my dear friend Vicky Hamilton going on 40 years now. Historically in a town like Hollywood, that's no small feat. But we're lucky, because even though it's the entertainment capital of the world where people have been coming for over a century to Be Somebody, Vicky, along with myself, and a large group of others, have managed to put art & creativity before business. We have always followed our hearts. I have watched Vicky follow her heart, and in doing so, I have had a front row seat to witness Vicky's inspiring and beautiful evolution; from a small-town girl, with a dream in her heart, a whole lot of courage, and a ton of moxie, against all odds, become one of the first and most successful Manager/A&R women in the record industry. And while discovering talent and making stars out of a lot of people, Vicky has become a star in her own right. And her star is only beginning to shine. Because it's now Vicky's turn. We should all keep an eye on her because there's so much more to come. I admire Vicky for her endless tenacity, and her passion and vision for her own art, whether it's her paintings, writing songs, or writing poems, she's got stories to tell. She tells them with grit and bite, honesty, sensuality, and softness. And she tells them all on her own terms. Vicky knows what she wants, and there's no stopping her. As she puts it so aptly in her poem by the same name, "I'm a Thunderstorm." And she is just that. This book of poems written in a 50-year span, from age 16 to present day, showing her growth and development as a writer, is just the tip of the iceberg of what to expect from her. But it's all Vicky... and read closely, these are tales of historic proportions, that will live on long after we are all gone.

— Iris Berry, author, editor, and publisher at
Punk Hostage Press

Introduction

My love affair with the written word started in junior high school. It was the early 70's, in New Haven, Indiana. The art and music of the time lead us youngsters to believe that peace, love and freedom were abound and that words had the power to change things. At the time, I had a very eccentric, entertaining English/ Creative Writing teacher named Larry Huff. Mr. Huff would read us poetry from the greats, then slide in a couple of his own. I was in awe of him, he showed the class how most songs probably started as poems. After turning in assignment one day, Mr. Huff stopped me and said how magnificent my last piece was and encouraged me to express my life in poetry, he made me believe my words mattered. I took this to heart and bought my first writing journal to record my thoughts. In a universe where I didn't feel heard, I could have my private thoughts and stash them away...hence this book, a lifetime of writing poetry.

In the debauchery of 1981, I moved to Hollywood, California to chase my dream of becoming the best rock band manager in the world. Dealing with big city life, misogyny of the record business, writing became my solace, my way of working through my problems. Rock n Roll, Metal and Glam bands became my obsession as a manager and an A&R person. I had a backstage pass to the underbelly of sex, drugs and narcissism. Being a woman in a man's business world, proved to be the object of a lot of my pain. I believed in the healing power of music so much, I put up with a lot of emotional abuse. I clearly was not a victim, I was a volunteer, writing poetry helped me make sense of it all.

Starting a new love affair? Looking at the potential of this new relationship or a failed love affair? What better way to analyze what happened than writing a poem about it.

When I got sober in 2000, my whole life changed. I was no longer masking my feelings with drugs and alcohol. I basically ripped the band-aid clean off and started taking a deep dive into who I was at the core of my being. I wanted to be more authentically myself, I wanted more freedom in my life without feeling ashamed, I was willing to look at everything that kept me in bondage. Most of poems from the last two decades are about the self-discovery of this new adult Vicky with clarity, and in my opinion, my best work. Getting these feelings of hostility and betrayal off my chest, has helped me move forward. I am an optimistic person most days, however, being able to express my most painful feelings in written word has been a Godsend to me.

This will probably be the only poetry book I will ever release, so I wanted to cover a span of time which covers me at 15 through me at 66. I have started with the newest and travel back to my innocence.

I hope you relate and enjoy the poems! Here's wishing you a lifetime of dreams that come true and whatever is your passion, make it a reality. Live your best dream.

Best Wishes,
Vicky Hamilton

Table of Contents

1   Sunflower
3   Sharks & Snakes
5   Peahen Rising
7   The Business of Music Reflection
9   Hoops
11 Next Level
13 Praise for Groupies
15 I Will Take Care of You
17 I'm a Thunderstorm
19 Love for this Monkey
21 Heartbreaker
23 Snow & Stars
25 Tryst
27 Trust
29 Ghost Notes
30 Triggered
33 My Rent a Husband
35 Cutter
37 The Legend
39 David Said
41 Flash Paper
43 Dog is God Backwards
44 Sad in Sobriety
47 Stir the Ice
49 The Crow
51 When in Rome
53 Venice Italy
55 The Fall in Venice
57 She's a Weapon
59 The Nothing Moments
61 The Woman's Worth
63 Broke and Broken
67 Pandemic
69 Mirrors
70 2LA

73   Your Ghost
75   Affluent Archer
76   Drink Me Up
79   Searching for Clues
81   Totems
83   Silence
85   Pure
86   Fuse my Muse
89   Goodbye
91   Everything's Over (Passion Crimes)
92   Star Collector
95   Tales of Emotions
97   The Pure Heart of my Mother's Love
99   In Anger
101   Let me Be Your Ocean
105   Meaning
107   Clouds
109   Mr. Natural
111   Time
113   Peace

"Music is probably the only real magic I have
encountered in my life. There's not some trick involved
with it. It's pure and it's real. It moves, it heals, it
communicates, and it does all these incredible things."

Tom Petty

2022 - 2024

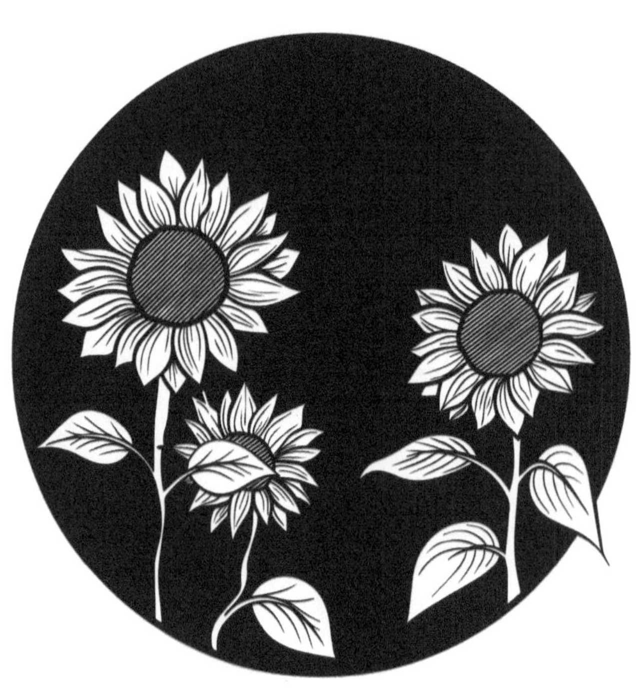

Sunflower
Vicky Hamilton

I am a Sunflower.
Sturdy at the base,
Supplying courage to persevere.
Bright, yellow and jagged on the outside,
The side I show the world.
Crazy and creative,
yet a dark abyss on the inside,
Showing vulnerability and fearfulness.
Somehow still spiritual.

Bright and dark,
I have a lionheart.
But may cut you down to size,
If you threaten my beloved art.

I always follow the sun...
I'm only inspired by love.

I am a Sunflower.

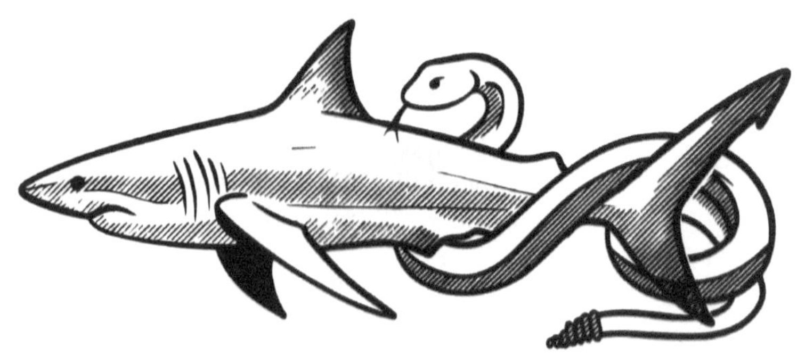

Sharks & Snakes
(And Other Animals)
Vicky Hamilton

Throw me in the snake pit,
Where I am numb from poisonous venom.
Chop me up into little bloody squares,
And feed me to the sharks, for a mid-day snack.

Live and learn,
As this is an entertainment tell-all,
I know there is no loyalty...
It's all just target practice,
Better make sure you are legally bullet proof,
While wearing a heart made of stone.

It's a cutthroat business,
Where grinning laughing hyenas,
Give you the Riddler's smile.
Charming conniving leopards,
Pretend to change their spots,
Just for a short time,
Until they walk away with your jackpot.

But never be the victim,
Instead, be the three monkeys...
Hear, see and speak no evil.
It's all fun and games,
There are no rules,
Just be the victor at all costs,
Then exit with a parade wave.

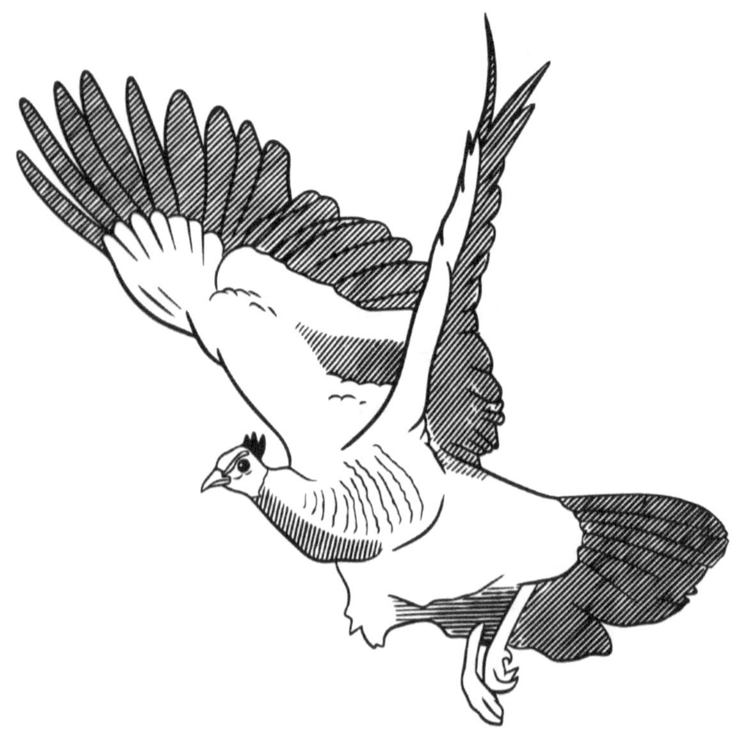

Peahen Rising
Vicky Hamilton

Rising from the ashes,
Of reflective discontent.
Your expectations are not a match,
For your narcissistic narrow bent.

Time to get a wider mirror,
So that I can examine the cracks.
Holly says musicians are my kryptonite,
But I am so much wiser now,
In the game of fight or flight.

The music business isn't about art.
This business is like all others,
It's about the beans they count...
Grind yours for that expensive cappuccino,
Because that is probably all you are going to get,
While you are muddling your thoughts,
Dreaming of pink clouds of happiness.

Money and trust,
Hardly ever make fair trade,
But if you have a crafty lawyer,
The fine print might warrant you gain.

Knowledge and Hope,
Make strange bedfellows.
The past is always lying-in wait,
To rewrite the narrative.
But if you seek the truth,
You will hear the clarity within these words,
I whispered in your ear,
While telling you this cautionary tale.

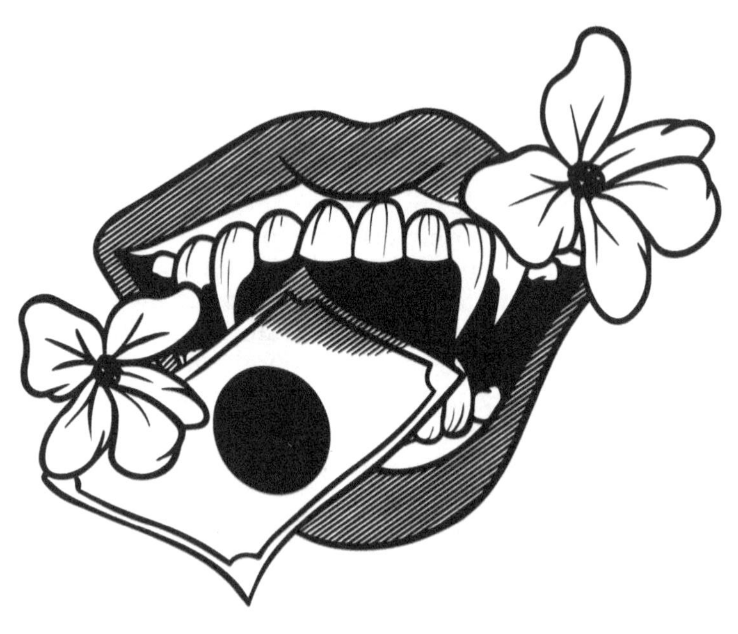

The Business of Music Reflection
Vicky Hamilton

In the middle of the meltdown,
I heard the voice deep inside,
Screaming "I've survived far worse than this.
Vampires, Liars and thieves,
Can't sink their teeth in me."

To your comment,
"You are a threat to the industry,
Because you are so outspoken."
Really?
That's all you got to pin on me?
I am supposed to be the shrinking violet,
In the assassination of my character?

No...I will stand tall,
In the eye of the storm.
I believe in the muse of the music,
Not the numbers on your social score card.

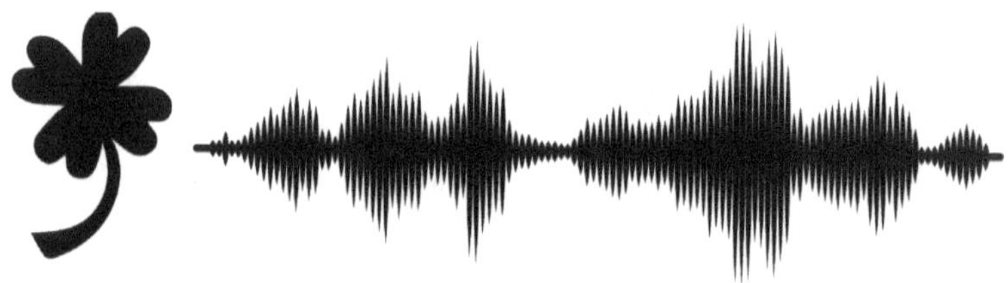

Hoops
Vicky Hamilton

It seems I'm always jumping through hoops,
Trying to prove my worth as a manager, executive
or a lover.
I'm only as good as my last performance,
Always begging to be paid, for the work I've already
done.

My male counterparts,
Work less, but have more success,
Sitting on a pot of gold, failing upward,
As they polish their golf game.

I'm lucky...
I have several supporters on my team,
They make sure I'm legally and karmically protected.
A few are even men...
Some mamas have raised them right,
To not see gender or color but judged by
who does the best job.

These days I feel ageism more than anything,
Hey young people!
You don't get stupid with age.
You learn a lot with time.
A sampling of what I've learned,
I must protect my heart and bank account,
As I'm the only one,
Taking care of myself.

But hey, I try and be fair,
If your art is brilliant,
I will dance with you....
Don't forget what you have promised and signed.
I will do what I agreed to,
Then we can hula hoop together.

Dig...?!
Win / Win

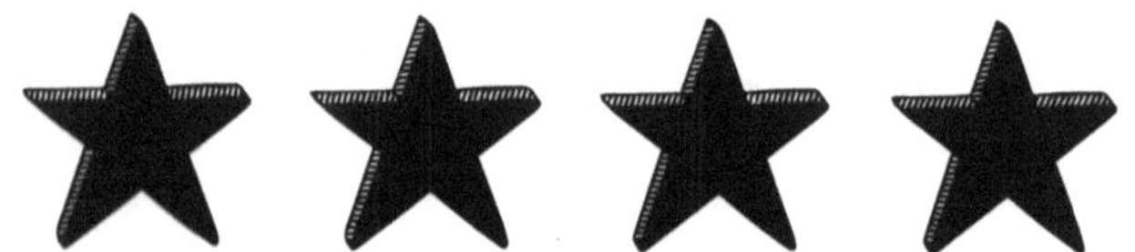

Next Level
Vicky Hamilton

It's that moment just before they break.
The crowds are coming,
I hear the girls talking in the bathroom about them.
They have "it", Whatever "it" is.....

I feel compelled to tell them all the pitfalls
of the business;
Don't accept drugs, don't drink too much...
Be true to your own aesthetic
And
Don't say yes to deals without reading the fine print.

In this moment, time stands still.
They know it all...
Hopefully my whispers sink in.
It's an exciting time,
Just before their fifteen minutes of fame.
Perhaps they will be the ones to headline arenas
and master fame.
I hope they will be the ones,
To win the game.

I pray for the right song, the prefect label and agent.
That these boys will fire on all cylinders,
As they pop up in their numbers,
I pray they really want to live up,
To the next level.

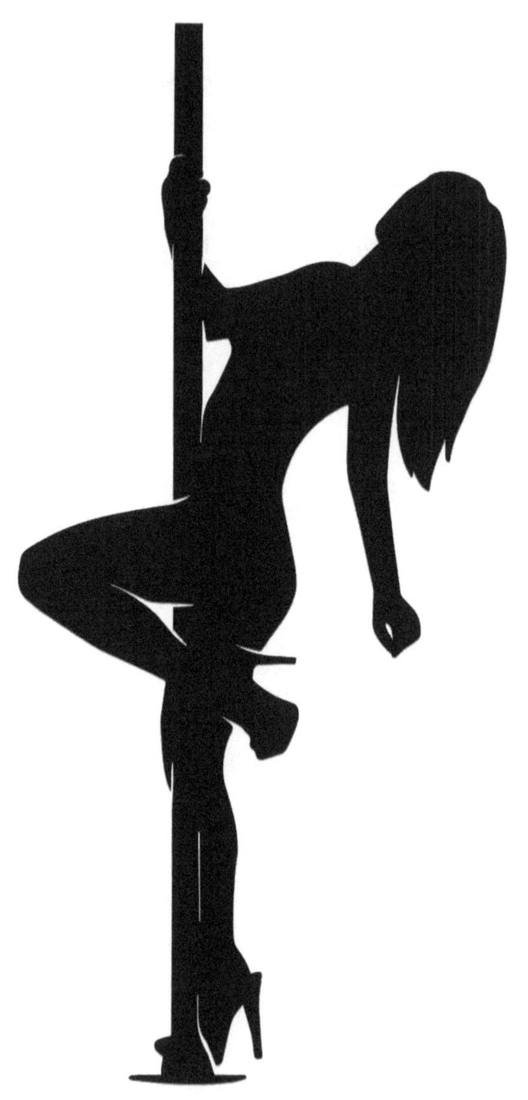

Praise for Groupies
Vicky Hamilton

I have always been grateful to groupies and strippers.
Groupies have always taken care of my bands,
Both sexually and financially.
These girls always figure out a way,
To pick up the guys when they are stranded,
Feed them when they are hungry,
And work out their sexual tensions.

These girls are always there for a light of their smoke,
And to buy a pack when needed...

We must praise the sex workers!
They improve Rock God's state of mind...
Keep us hard working women from getting raped,
And perhaps freeing up an evening for us to have a
date.

But Ladies...
Please don't give my bands,
Drugs, Alcohol or STD's...
Also try and keep your own self clean.
Don't tell them they are the best of the best,
Or tell your private affairs to the press!

I will gladly hand the boys over to you,
For days when they are not working or touring.
Thank you for building up their egos,
This keeps them going...
Please just don't chase them down a rabbit hole,
Try to return them better than you found them.

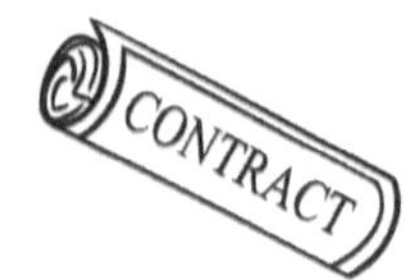
CONTRACT

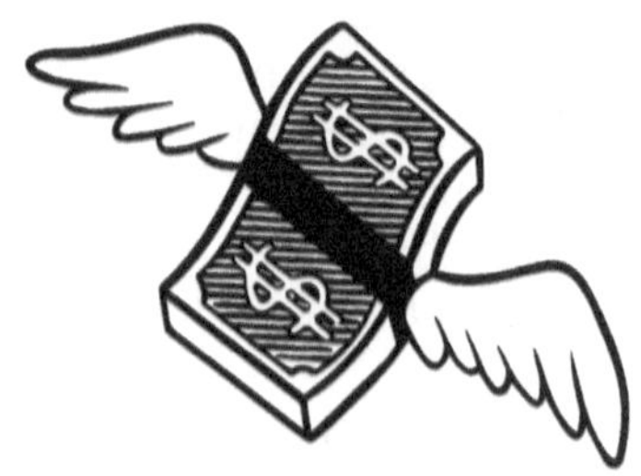

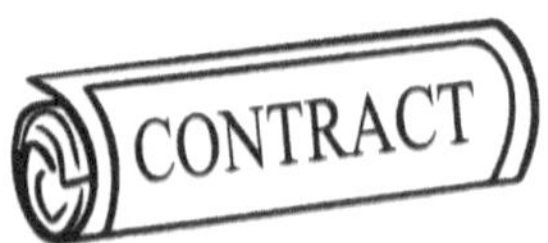
CONTRACT

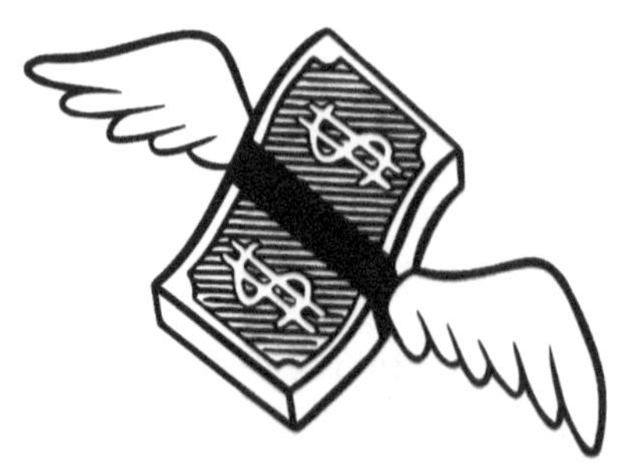

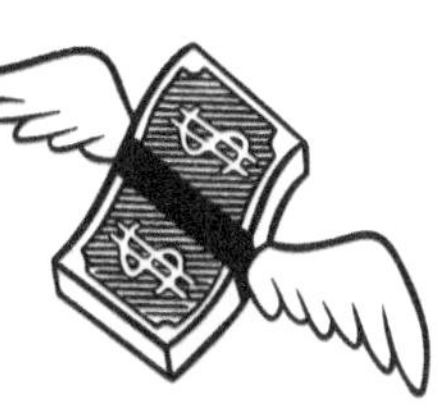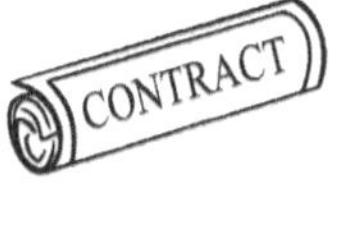

I Will Take Care of You
Vicky Hamilton

I wish I had a dollar
For every time an artist said,
"When I make it, I will take care of you."

Axl said it, Brett too...
Many who didn't make it as well...

Now when I hear these words,
I shudder...

Please don't say it...
Whether you think it is true or not,
You won't.

Today you don't need to say it,
My lawyer will now wrap you tightly in paper...
This is how I take care of myself.

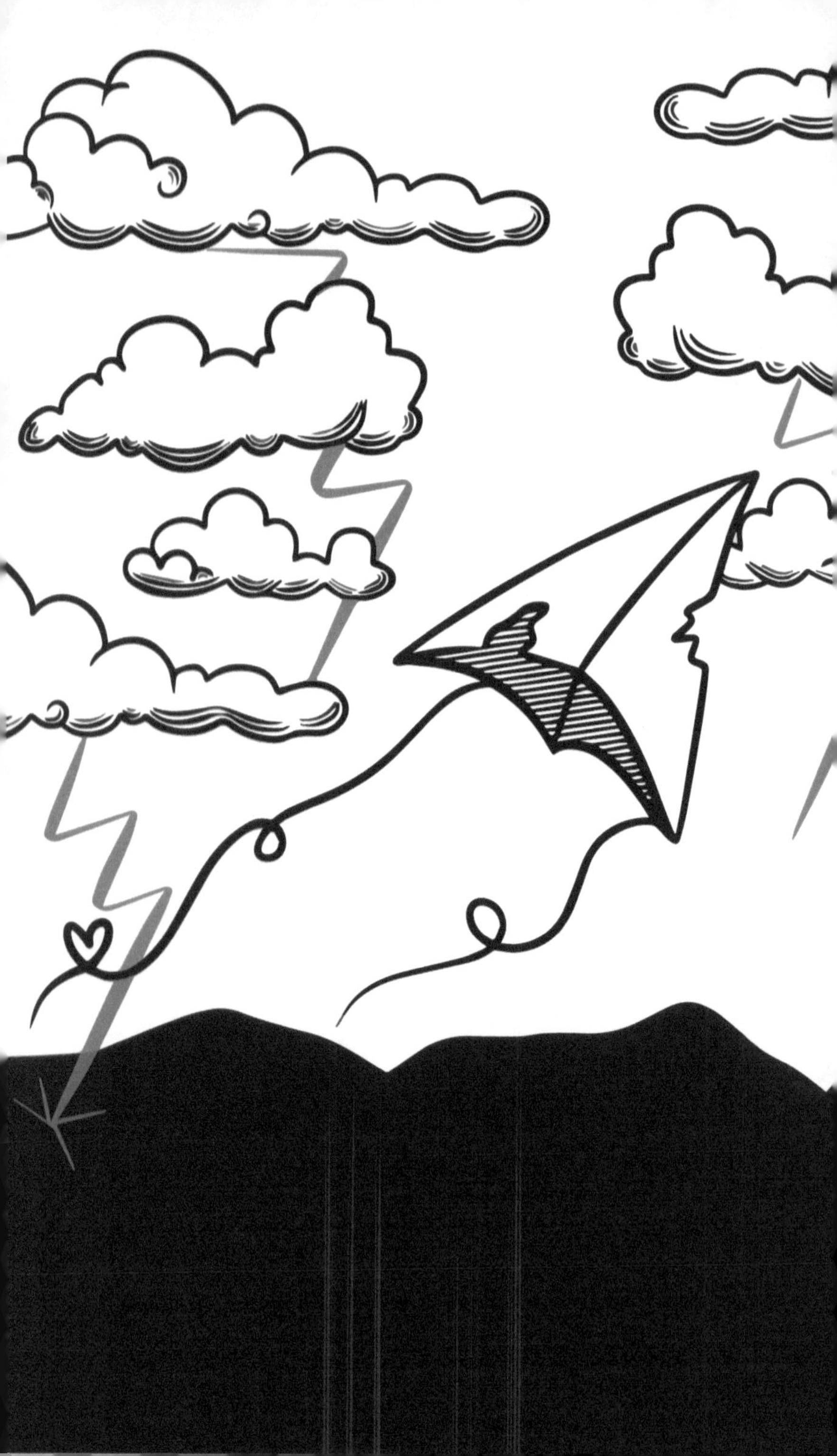

I'm a Thunderstorm
Vicky Hamilton

I'm lost like August Rush,
Following the music,
Hoping to find my home.

The notes fill the air,
Whirling, spinning yet turnkey,
Pressing stars with a wind battered kite in the night,
I listen and pray,
Galvanizing dreams that magically manifest.

Lightening,
Followed by a thunderous boom,
The rain pours down
Then rises back up,
Penetrating fame,
Then is lost once again.

It's a romantic notion,
The roar of the ocean,
The calling of the lion heart,
Passion pierces the heart of creativity,
Somehow symphonic yet alone.

Moving in quickly,
Leaving the same way,
For the artists in my wake,
I'm a Thunderstorm.

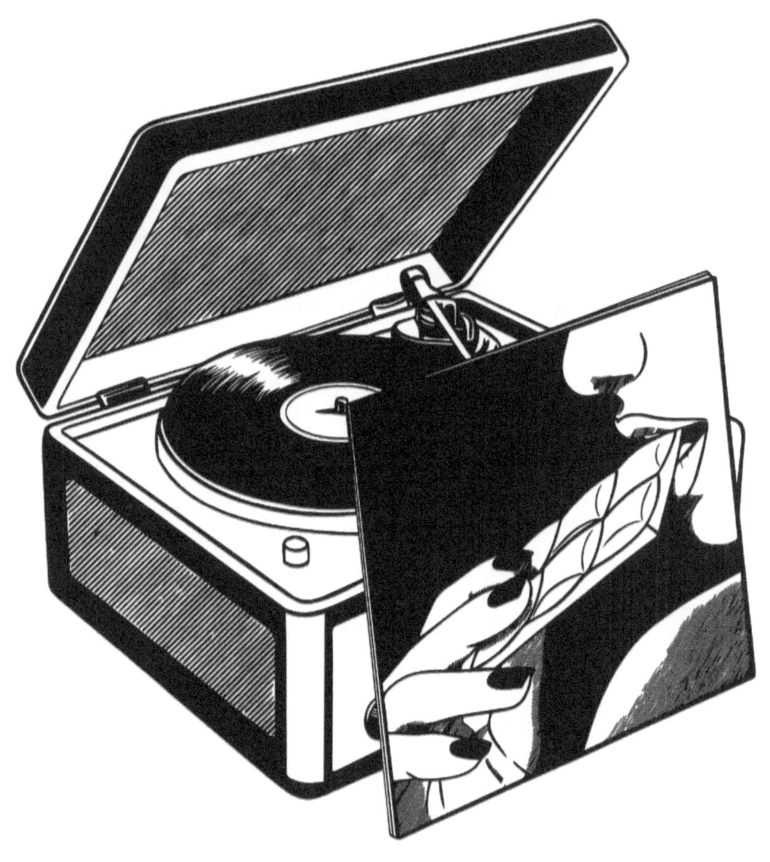

Love for this Monkey
Vicky Hamilton

Alex is always there for me.
All I must do is hit play.
Who needs a real lover anyway?
I can take a magical oral trip with him anytime,
His lips move slowly,
As he says exactly the right things.

Oxytocin, Dopamine releases...
just from hearing his voice...
As the low volume, whispers in my ear.
Add in a tasty chocolate bar,
And the weekend romance is epic,
Without a blow- up doll.

So what if it's just a fantasy?
This visualization is hard to beat.
Better than being disappointed by average Joe Schmo,
Or a boring discussion with a Bumble date.
He's always on time,
And it doesn't cost a dime.
He's got all the right moves,
And I don't have to leave my bedroom.

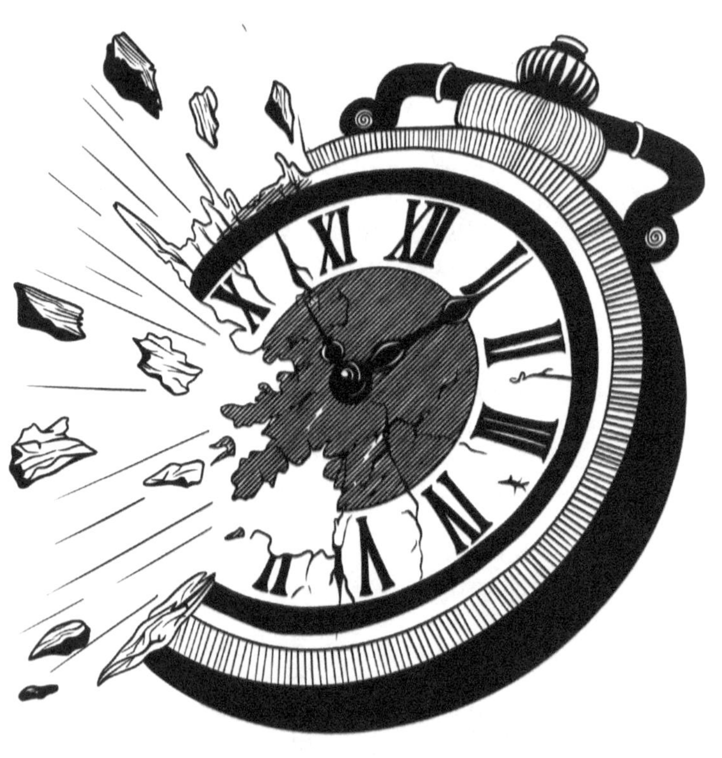

Heartbreaker
Vicky Hamilton

This girl who was obsessed with Petty,
And sold Damn the Torpedoes to everyone
who would listen.
That girl could do and did everything.
No fear,
Just faith that the universe would act on her behalf.

I still follow my own bliss,
However, I weigh the pros and cons a bit more.
Can we have it all?
No, not really.....
You must choose the most important things,
As the clock runs out...

I never though the day would come,
That I would outlive my heroes,
Petty, Bowie and Prince
Now my friends are dying too...

I hope I get a glimpse
Of at least one true love,
Before I leave this planet...
So I know this ride wasn't just a game.

Hot sex is nothing,

If the heart doesn't sing.

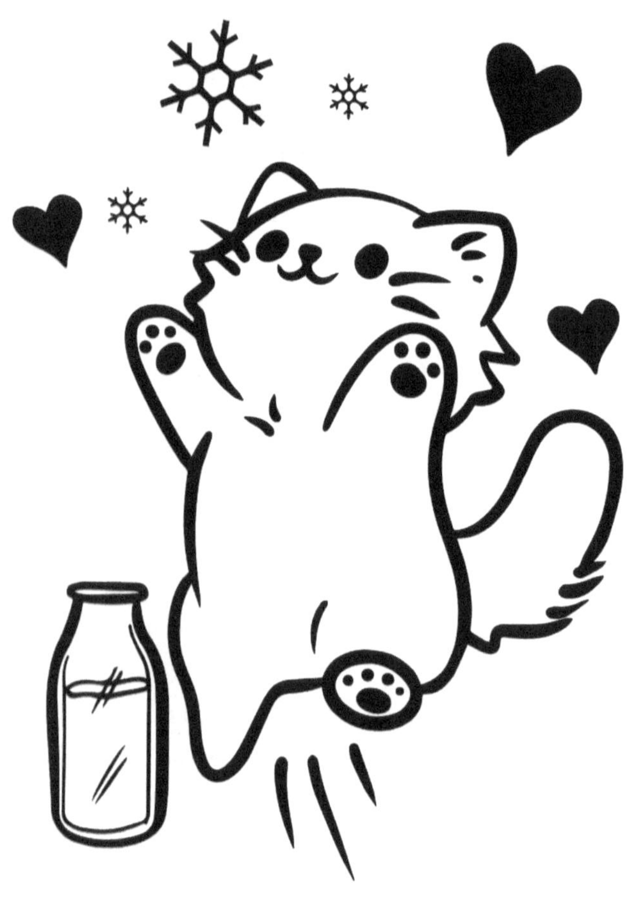

Snow & Stars
Vicky Hamilton

You are fresh as new fallen snow,
I am a old soul,
The last shooting star...
Perhaps, star crossed lovers is closer,
We still glitter
As light on a mirror ball.

We coo and flutter, Wings of a Dove.
Hold the magic, not the fear.
We can only accept our vulnerability,
When we can acknowledge our pain,
True forgiveness is the gift that sets us free.

I don't want to break or jade you,
However, I must be myself.
Unfortunately, I don't trust easily.
Patience and Passion are the winning game.
A mixed bag; herbs, sugar, and spice,
Which take time to blend,
Together we are sun baked iced tea.

Be gentle, my sweet
Like the milk breath of a kitten...
You can have it all.
Light the fire if you dare.
Throw caution to the gale.
Fan the fire of this little storm.
Just choose the sky and stay,
While Bowie sings Wild is the Wind.

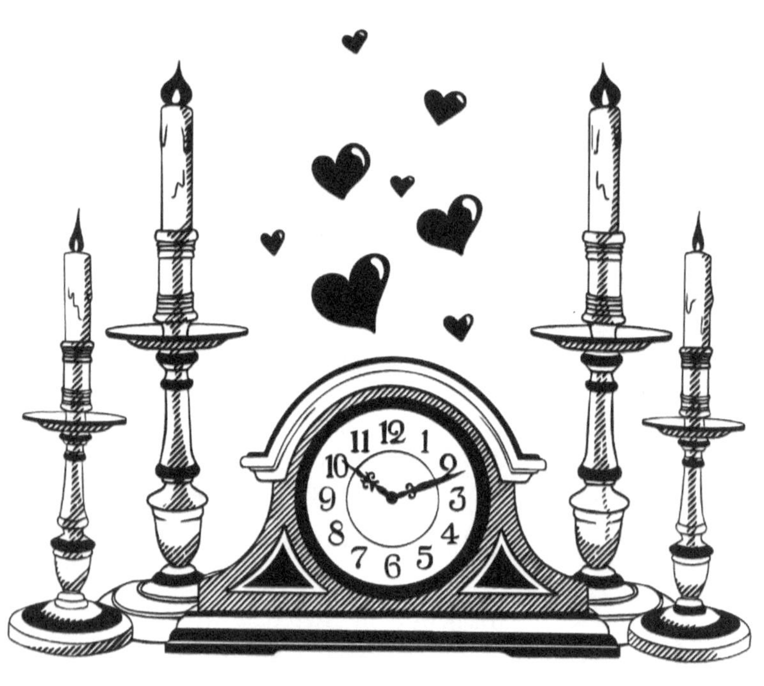

Tryst
Vicky Hamilton

I swim in your pools of blue,
I drown in your infinite sadness.
Across the dinner table,
We reach for our dreams,
Within each other's minds...

Making our own fireworks,
On the bed where we intertwine.
Naked honesty comes to a head,
I allow myself to trust,
This love transcends time and space,
Whether it last or not.

I just want you to be happy...
I will always hold this space for you.
In my memory, we exist in a veil of ecstasy,
Between hot summer night sheets, glowing candles and
stolen clocks.

The promise of this lover's tryst,
Will always live in my heart.

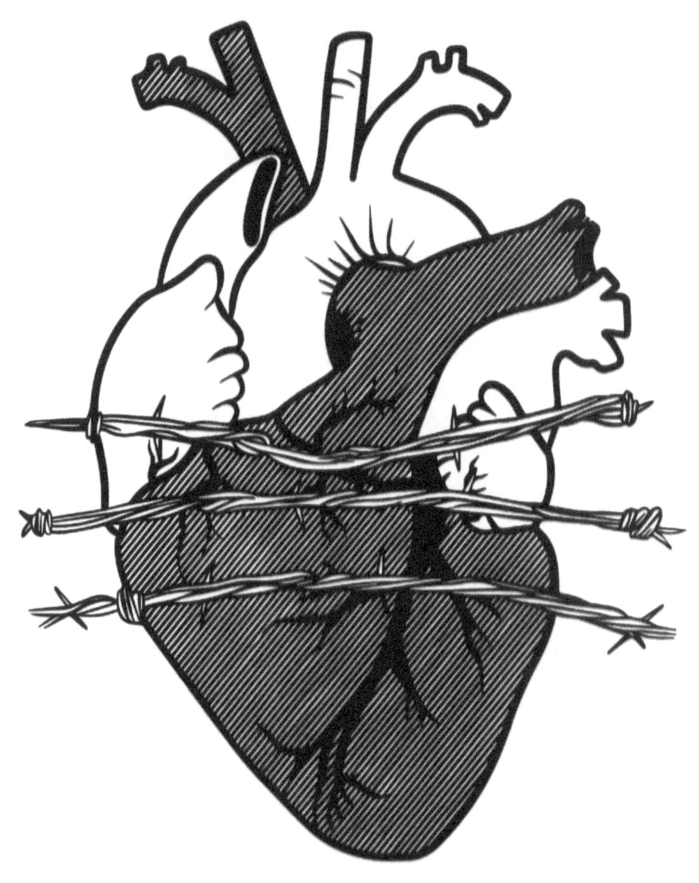

Trust
Vicky Hamilton

I have always been,
An all or nothing kind of girl.
Passion and inspiration run hot,
For this Aries

When you showed up,
I took everything very slow…
As if you might be the last,
Or the knowing that you could potentially
Stomp on my heart with hobnail boots.

Still, I threw caution to the wind,
I handed you my heart, body and soul.
Telling myself,
I must be open…for love to show up.

Only on the other side of the door,
To find unrequited love…
You said my love was healthy …
Then you disappeared,
Like it never happened.

Trust?!
Yeah, I really did.
However, I probably never will again.
At least I forgot about the others before you…
Now I am your mirror… lonely, sad and depressed.
It's better to be skeptical and expect nothing.
While installing a protective barbwire fence around my
heart.

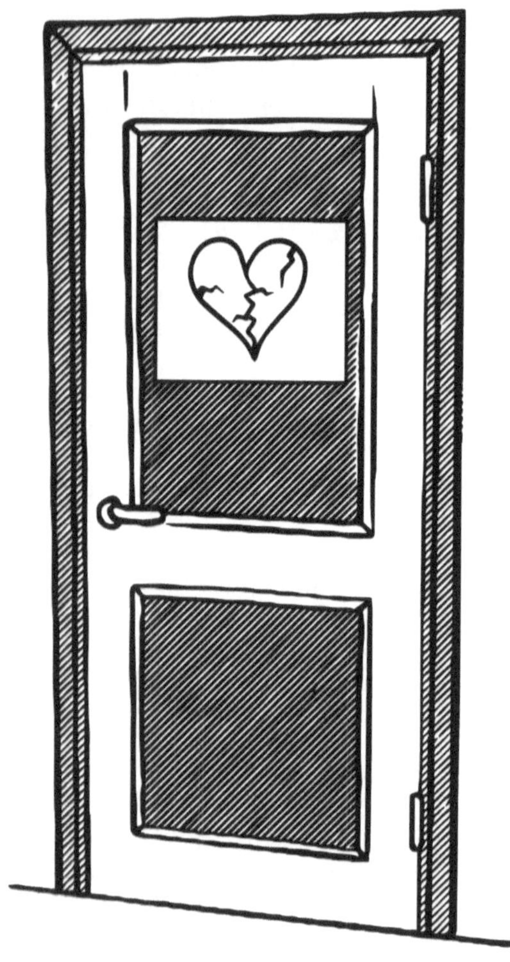

Ghost Notes
Vicky Hamilton

I'm bleeding out...
Trying to get to the bottom of the grief,
Of losing you.
In your ghosting, it's almost like you died.
Yet, I occasionally see a social post of you and some
pussycat.

I told you I loved you,
And
You couldn't handle "healthy love",
Saying only that you were on a different level,
Which made no sense to me,
Since I only asked for fidelity.

Choosing to walk away, Into the night,
Like the ghost you are now,
In my life.

I see you in my dreams, in cars on the road.
I talk with you in my mind,
Replaying every scene,
Looking for clues.
I wish I understood,
What made you disappear.

It's cruel to not allow me closure.
I trusted you,
To be gentle with my heart.
I gave you the best I have,
But I guess my best, was not good enough.

Was the conquest what you wanted all along?
I was probably doomed, in the beginning,
When you knocked on my door.
If God is watching,
Will he let you into heaven?
Knowing you broke my heart...
Karma has a way of coming back,
Like a boomerang in the fog.

Triggered
Vicky Hamilton

Something always stops me
In my tracks,
From telling you how I really feel.
Memories of relationships long ago,
And how the ending,
Was the devastation of me.

The years have passed,
And I am feeling stronger.
I pause before speaking
And take off my armor.
My faith is greater,
Then the fear that you will leave me.

Because I'm triggered,
Your words push all my buttons
I feel my temperament rise
I want to fight or flight,
But I'm coming in for a landing
And holding this love tight.

We are all made of stardust,
But God gave you an extra kiss.
The bullet in your gun,
Is your empathic vision.
I see the seriousness in your eyes
The determination, the drive,
The voice of affliction.
Your shine could blind this world,
If you would only let it.

I want to really hear you,
Be your mentor and your guide.

I see the light within you,
And know you will one day shine.
Life keeps bringing us the same lessons,
Until we pass the test,
I think you'll be legendary and iconic,
Probably my best.

I won't let you trigger me.
I won't let my temperament rise,
I won't fight or flight,
I'll come in for the landing
And hold this love tight.

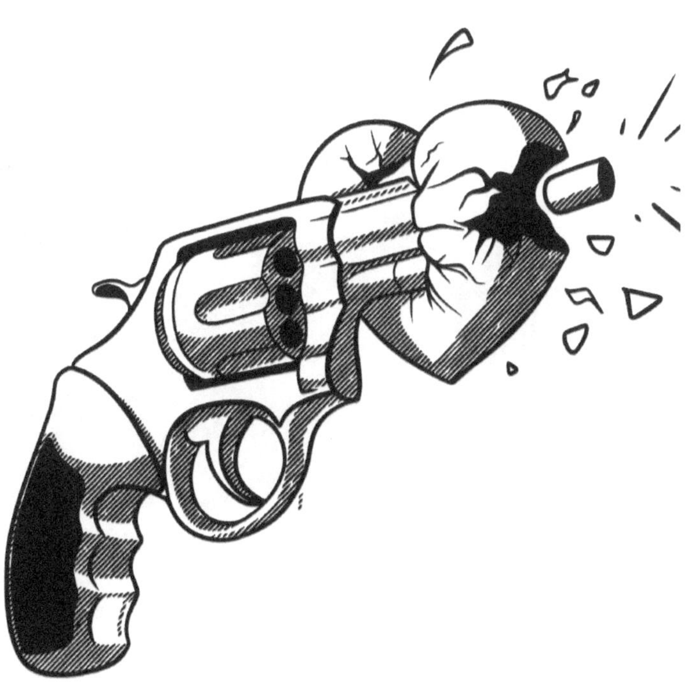

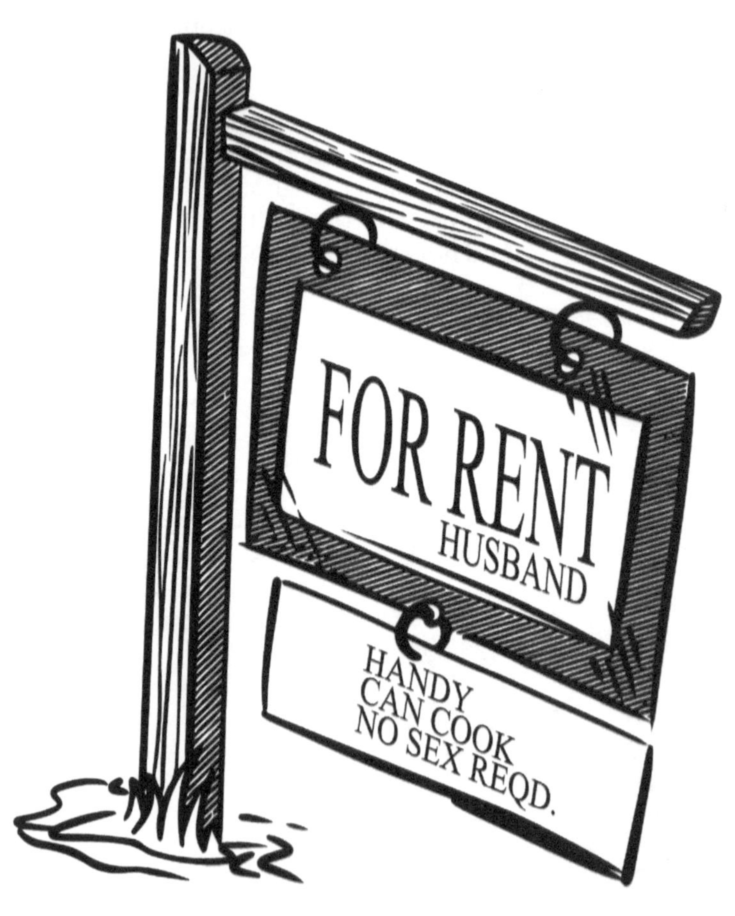

FOR RENT
HUSBAND
HANDY
CAN COOK
NO SEX REQD.

My Rent a Husband
Vicky Hamilton

My rent a husband can fix it all,
Except a broken heart.
But he will joke with me,
Until I laugh at myself.
Then will help me hang pictures of my past,
On my wall.

He barbecues like a dream,
Debates opposing political views,
Tells me about the bands he absolutely hates,
And
Defends terrible movies.

He makes me laugh,
Has a great shoulder to cry on.
Doesn't expect me to do;
His laundry, dishes or pick up his messes.

It's a minimal commitment,
With honesty and light heartiness,
It's a true love,
A real friendship,
We don't have to agree...
Or have sex.

Like adults with infant children,
I can send him home,
Whenever I please,
Then jump into bed with my Beagle pups,
For emotional safety.

Living the dream.
Free and easy.

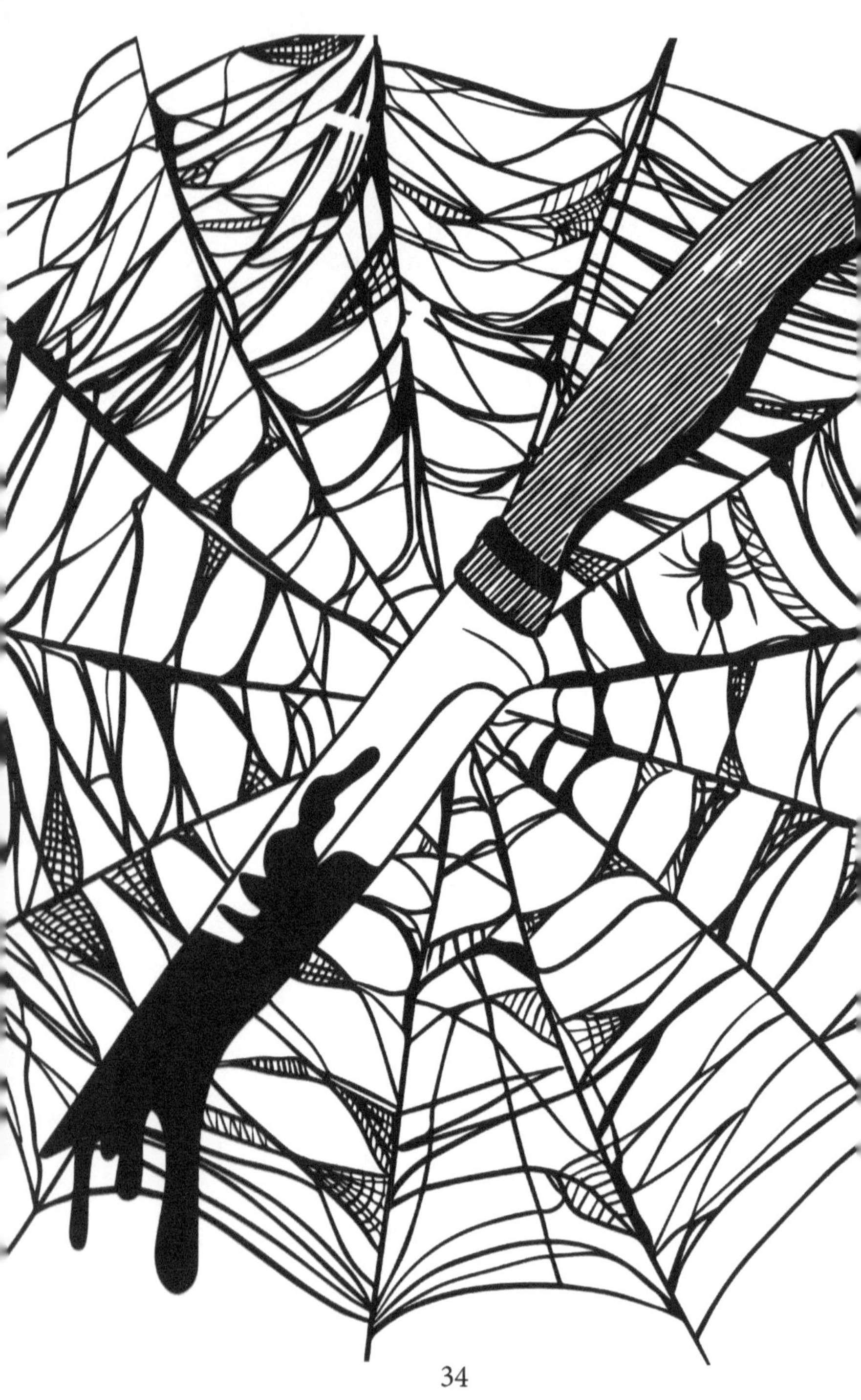

Cutter
Vicky Hamilton

He's an emotional cutter,
Can't feel unless there is pain.
No amount of caring or wisdom,
Can stop the bloodletting.
He will have to find the courage,
To do this for himself.

Blame is a game
He loves to play...
He is never guilty,
A victim, caught in his own web...
The he said, and she did,
Makes you feel the knife within your back.
The lies he tells everyone,
Were created in his own head.

Take your litany of literary poison
And make me the villain of yet another tale.
Use up every drop, until there is no more,
Only then will you look around and notice,
You are all alone.

In the meantime,
I will take lemons and make lemonade.
For California sunshine
Always returns after the rain.
Beautiful and clean,
Like the serenity prayer.

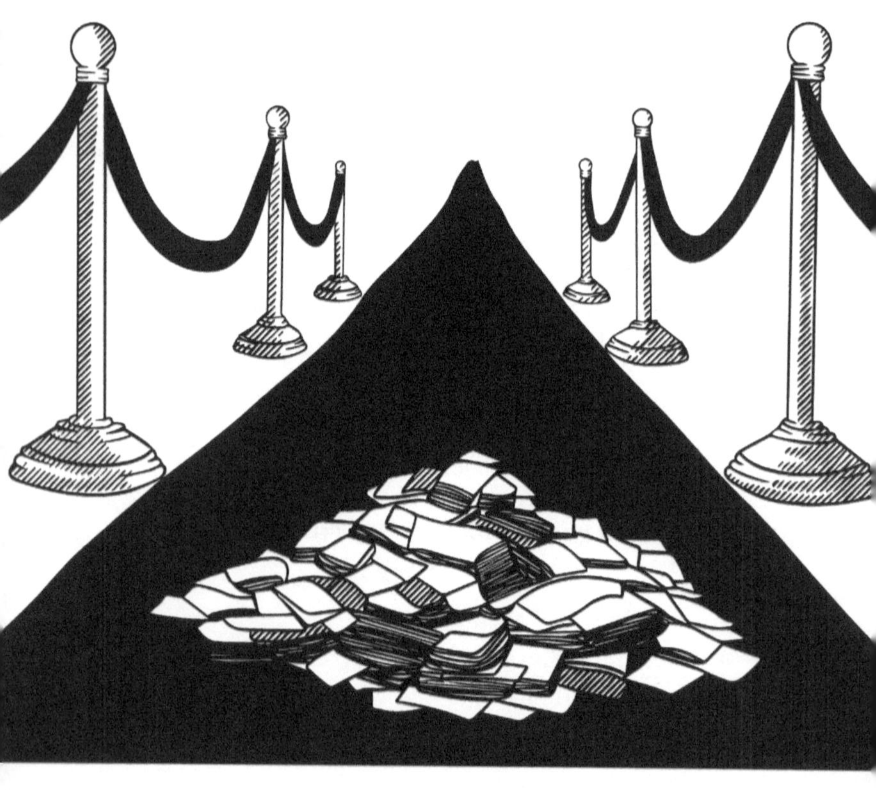

The Legend
Vicky Hamilton

I will not crawl on the red carpet to reach you.

However,
Every time you take a bow,
I hope I sneak across your memory.
Remember how I housed you,
When the cops were looking for you?
How I told all the record labels,
You were the next big thing.
Many have come and gone,
In these forty years...
Just pulled another knife out of my back today,
From a young band who thinks they know everything.
Not a surprise,
But still disappointing.
A few good shows,
And they imagine slaying all the industry dragons.

But you,
My red-haired, green-eyed legend,
You really did it!
Cost me a lot of years of therapy,
Along with my distrust of all that followed.
I'd hoped you would one day make it right...
I guess while we are still both alive,
The fat lady isn't singing....

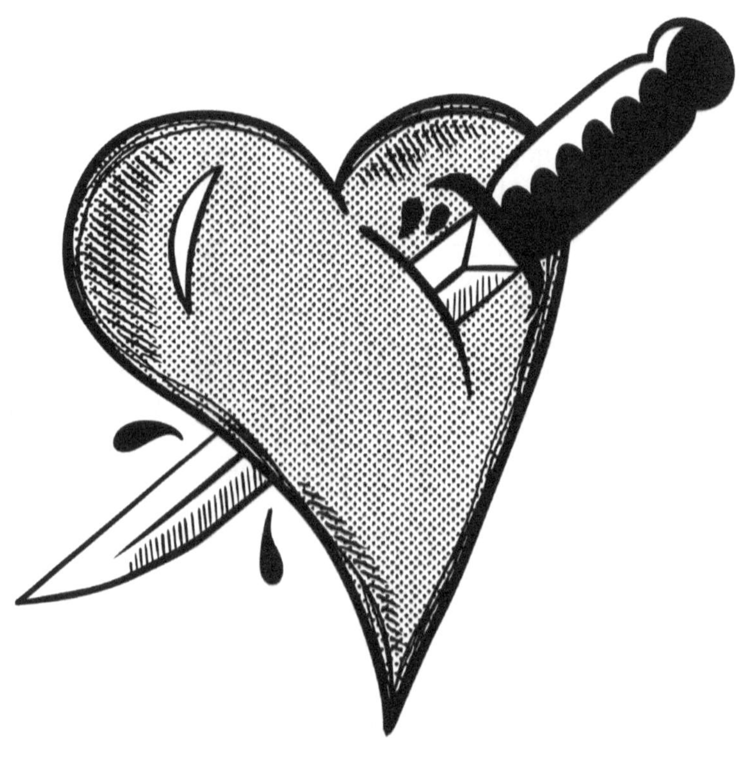

David Said
Vicky Hamilton

David said,
"If it was easy, everyone would do it."
Which turns out to be true.
Couldn't you have showed me the map to the
treasures,
How I should have navigated these mad waters?

David said,
"Don't play the victim"
Well yeah, I was young, dumb and obsessed with cum...
I will own my part in this,
I've really tried to evolve,
Take the pain and stay in the game.

David said,
"I'm not a mind reader, you have to tell me your
problems."
I have now learned the art of self -expression,
I rarely hold back,
Unless it will harm others.

David said,
"Every time you want to sign a band, it cost me a
million dollars."
Understood.
However, unless you take chances,
You never know.
What works and what doesn't.

David said,
"Be careful who you cross on the way up...
They will be waiting with long knives
on the way down."
True that...
Even just succeeding makes them lay in wait,
From my experience.

Thank you, David
For your truthful statements,
These life lessons I always carry with me.

Flash Paper
Vicky Hamilton

It's ok that you broke me.
It lets me know, I'm alive.
Cut so deep,
Sent me to the bottom of the cold blue ocean.

Makes me wonder,
Why I loved you?
In truth, it's been an alchemical fire,
Passion, love, anger and hate.

Just below the surface,
Looking up.
If it reaches the air,
It will ignite like flash paper.
Then just gone...Nowhere to be found.

I don't need you to torture me,
I can do that, all by myself.
Just unfinished business in my mind's memory.
The betrayal of the heart, aesthetic and art.
Let go, let go, let go.
Live and let live.

I'm shaking the dust off my wings,
And flying away.
Into a new day. New year, new life.
Perhaps, one last song.

Finished Now.

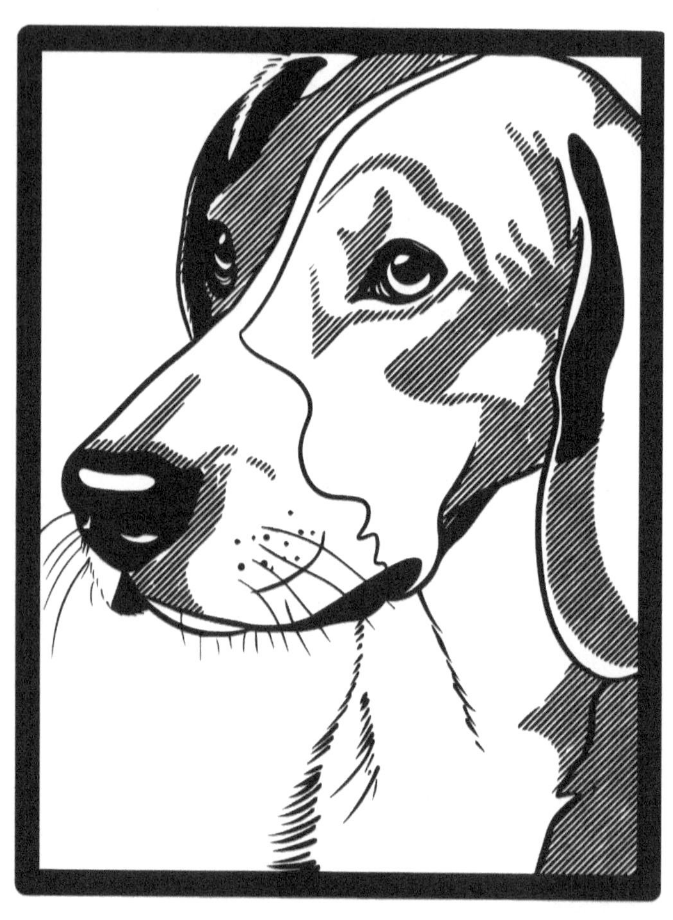

PLUTO

Dog is God Backwards
Vicky Hamilton

I was born in the year of the dog,
I'm loyal, forgiving, and sweet...
But like a dog,
I never forget.

Dog is God backwards,
So many life moments are born from puppy love.
Some days I feel like dogs are my only friends,
My dear Watson loved only me,
Having a fight with a client?
My sweet Pluto is there,
With a quick kiss and a cuddle.

So many miracles come to me,
Through dogs.
My best business and shopping spree deals,
The writer for my tv series,
Even backstage passes to The Kills,
All pup love inspired.

Yes, Dog is God backwards.

Sad in Sobriety
Vicky Hamilton

The mental valleys have low lows.
The upward skyrockets are the high highs.

Now that I feel all my feelings,
In the same day,
I can laugh my ass off,
And also breakdown and cry.

When I was young,
I never let myself feel.
I'd drink a Tanqueray and grapefruit,
And chase it down with pills.

Quaaludes were my favorite,
They made me love everyone.
Smoking was my best friend,
Cigarettes, pot, it didn't matter...
A long drag made me feel fashionable,
Never mind, it was clouding my thoughts and my
lungs.

It got to the point,
I couldn't breathe without wheezing.
I knew it was time to quit,
But I couldn't break the habit,
Until I knew it would kill me, if I didn't.

So I cried every day,
While I white knuckled sobriety.
I went to meetings,
Had a good sponsor,
I changed my life.
I tried to reinvent myself.
I was so raw on the inside,
I became really shy.

That was twenty -four years ago.
I am no longer triggered by people using around me.
My friends all changed,
I became a workaholic,
Began to over analyze everything.
At least, I never had hangovers.

It's so hard to stay sober,
Through a breakup,
Loss of clients,
And the death of a good friend, at the same time.
I'm doing it....
But I'm damn near out of mind.

I'm so fucking sad...
I question God about why?
I tell myself,
No rain, no rainbows.
I live to tell,
Another day,
One day at a time.

It's not easy...
As I remember everything.
I'm cut to the emotional quick,
However, I am grateful.
I can put my own arms around myself and squeeze.

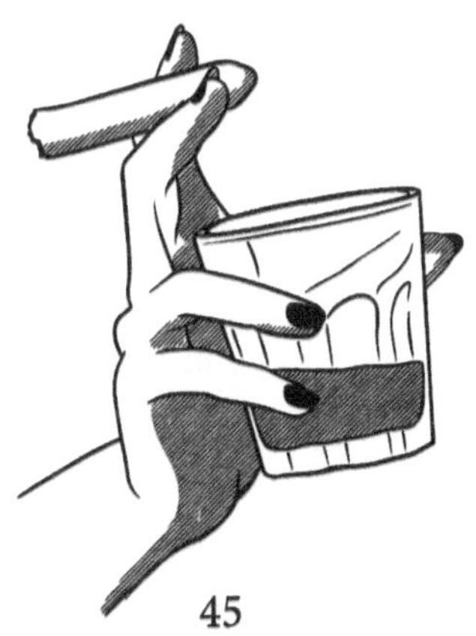

45

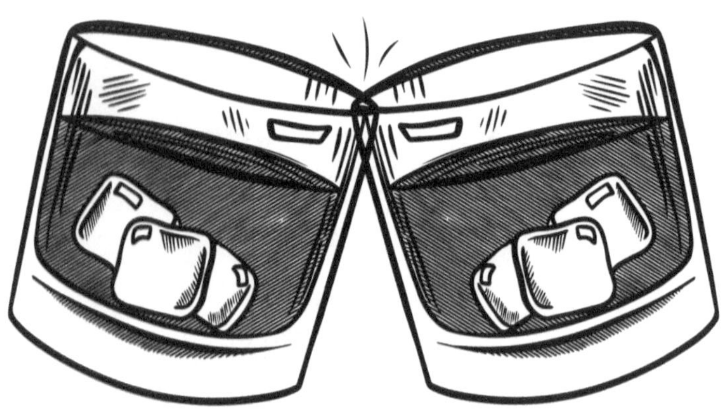

Stir the Ice
Vicky Hamilton

The words are stuck
In the back of my throat.
I want to take bait...
Let them come flying out.

Breathe, Breathe, Breathe
Shove the whole diatribe back down.

Look to the good.
Like his haunting laughing eyes.
Catch his gazes,
hold it right there- -
He nods his head,
As he stirs the ice with his fingers.

It feels like sex,
But it is not home.

Forget him yet forgive him...
That angry nun in my head whispers.
The best thing he ever had,
Is about to walk away.

Just know in every ending,
Comes a brand new beginning
With a shiny, charming protagonist.

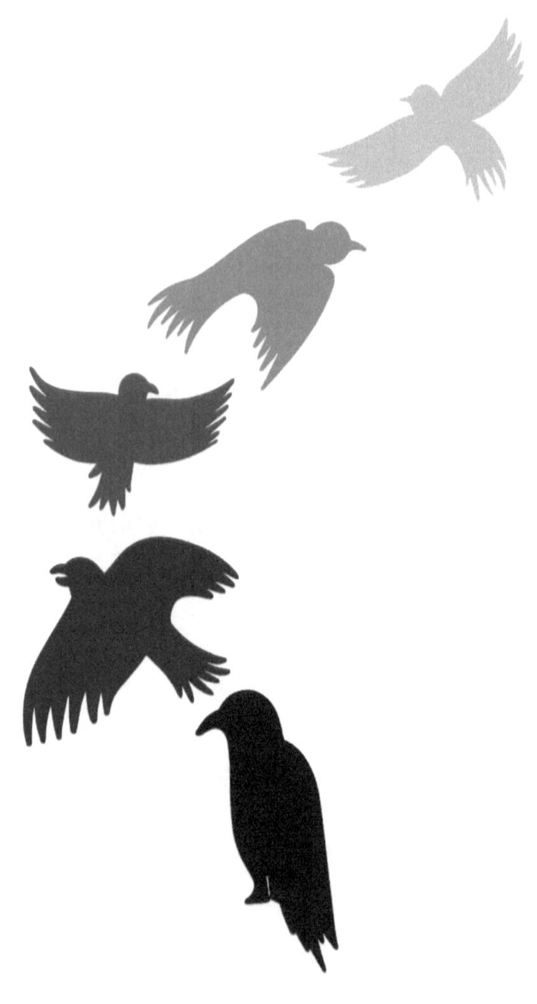

The Crow
Vicky Hamilton

I buried the crow in my yard,
After days of looking at it, from my kitchen window.
His murder buddies kept coming by and watching as...
I dug his grave.

That day,
My heart let you go.
A funeral for a friend.
I cried.
While the emotion welled up inside me,
Then was let go.

Funny, how the crows know.
They follow me on walks with the Beagles now.
Making those clicking sounds...
Ticking little clocks, they laugh,
And wait for your return.

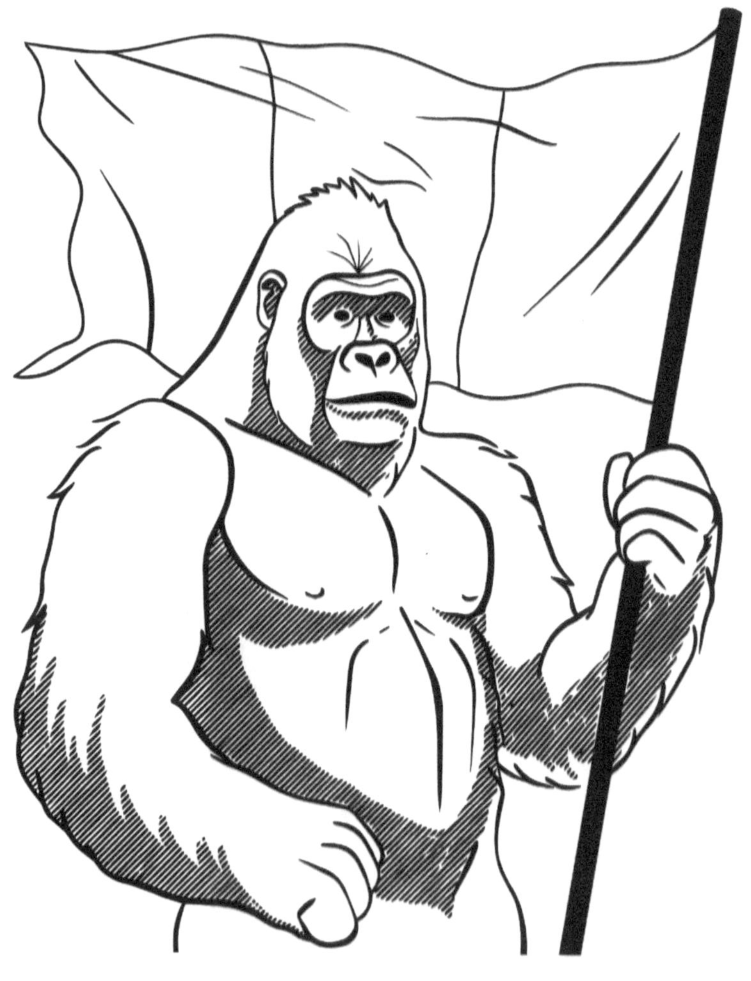

When in Rome
Vicky Hamilton

I'm in Rome,
Everything is so old here,
I feel young!
The Vatican, Colosseum, Pantheon...
Pasta, Gelatos, Cappuccinos...
Tourists, tourists, tourists!
I guess I am one as well.
Worshipping Italy at The Trevi Fountain,
Wash away my sins,
So many tourists,
I couldn't get close enough to toss a coin for three
days!

Walk, walk, walk,
Then walk some more....
It's great exercise,
This three-hundred-pound Gorilla, is pounding on my
head and chest,
A present from the Covid carrying kids,
Sitting by me on the plane,
I can't breathe.

Vacation?
I'm not sure I know how to do that...
I want to rest, turn off my head.
I can't, I won't, I can't,
I keep thinking of home...
Maybe, you must get away,
To know you have it made,
In your own backyard,
In your little corner of the world.

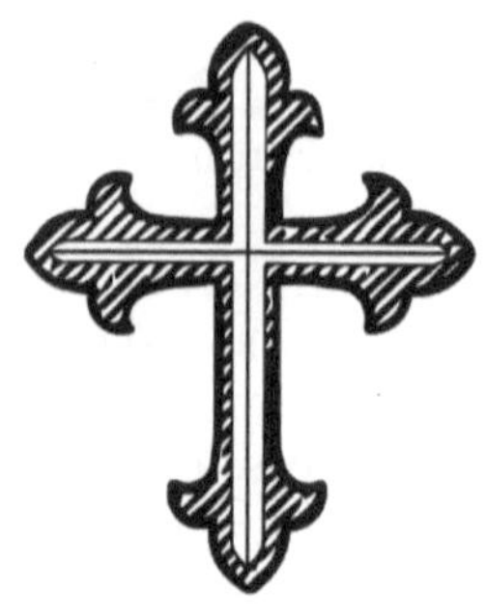

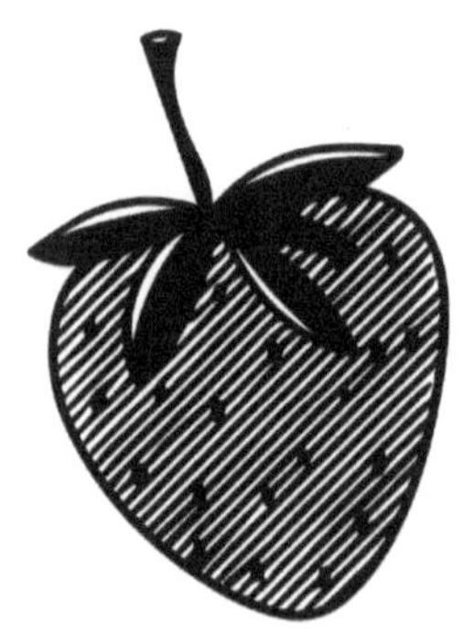

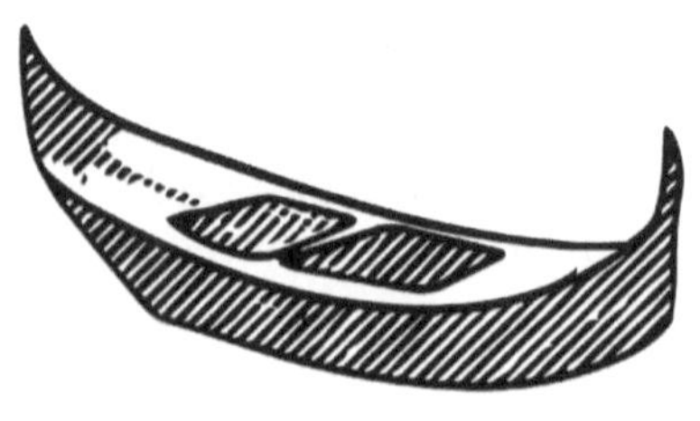

Venice Italy
Vicky Hamilton

Casanova lived here; an Aries like me.
It's a beautiful city.
So romantic,
With little hiding spots to steal a kiss.

Italianos really have mastered food.
Not just pasta,
Strawberries so dark red,
You know they taste good before you bite in.
I have fallen in love with pear juice too,
It's never been as sweet as it is in Venice.

The gondola ride...
I've dreamed about this since my teens.
Something so seductive about it.
I'm here in 2024, but it takes you back,
To the 1700's
Then further.

The Fall in Venice
Vicky Hamilton

When I fell down the marble staircase,
I knew it was the end.
The end of the Italian vacation,
The probable end of our friendship.

I picked myself up,
As I always do...
Didn't realize my wrist was broken,
Until sunrise in New York City the next morning.

Sometimes things are just meant to be over.
People change. Feelings severed.
I guess we are no longer like-minded.
Only our love of pasta remains.

Thanks for showing me Italy.
Yet another bucket list item, crossed off.
At least my head didn't bleed out,
Like those beautiful strawberries,
Tossed in the garbage.

Goodbye St. Mark's Square Basilica,
Delicious cappuccinos, blown glass and galloping
horses.
When the cast comes off in six weeks' time,
Maybe the beauty in my memory will remain.
Like the fantasy of Casanova's, passionate addicting
kiss.

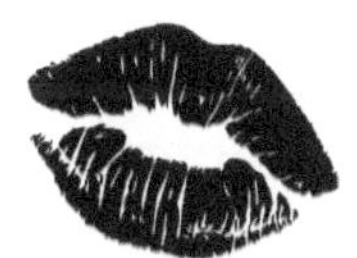

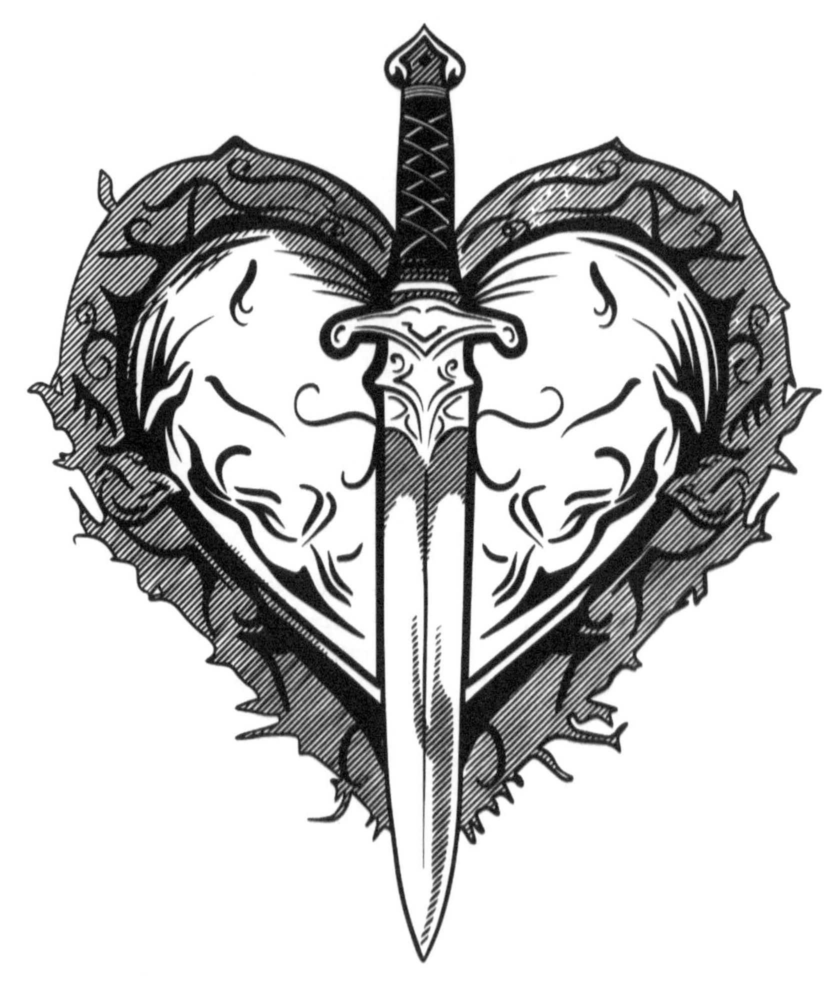

She's A Weapon
Vicky Hamilton

You like her,
And want to get closer.
So you engage her in conversation,
And cover your boner.

You have her cornered,
Your words fumble and fall.
You turn beet red,
And will say anything to get her to bed.
A whiff of her perfume
Takes you somewhere else.

She's a weapon,
Sharp as a knife.
She's a weapon,
She picks up on our deception.
She's a weapon,
She's going to teach you a lesson.

You are as sick as your secrets,
And as lost as your lies.
She has vision and clarity,
And will cut you down to size.
It's over,
Bang, bang...
You are as good as dead.
She's a weapon.

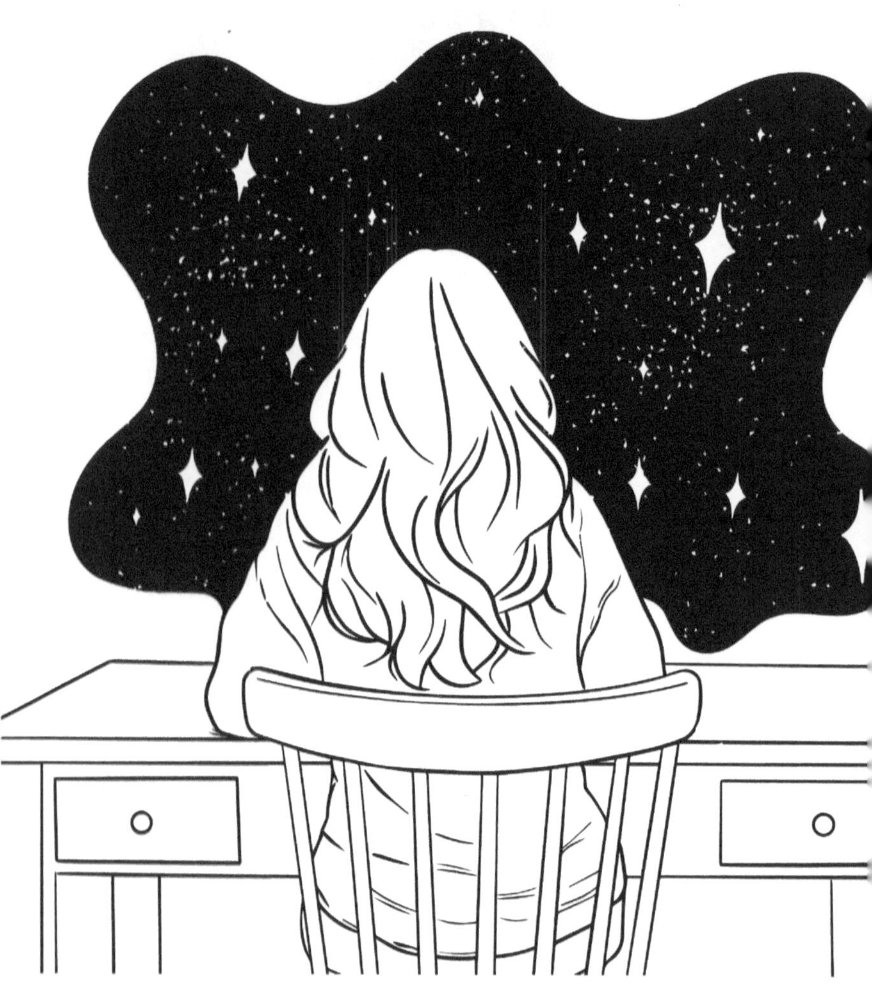

The Nothing Moments
Vicky Hamilton

Sometimes you must go away,
To get clarity.
Traveling has taught me a lot,
As much as I like to bitch about my clients...
I really miss them when they are out of reach.
Same with my friends.

I really love my life.
My work, my play, the tumbles in the sheets, my pups.
Mostly, my sobriety....
God within.
I guess it's true acceptance...
Of the real me.

I'm not like anyone else.
I'm original, like Mona Lisa.
Sometimes I can just, "be."
Not every moment has to be filled with something.

Nothing Is nice too...
Like the spontaneity in your lovers kiss and knowing
look.
Love the dream, you are dreaming,
As it soon will be your reality.
Recognize it when it shows up,
Be grateful,
In the nothing moments.

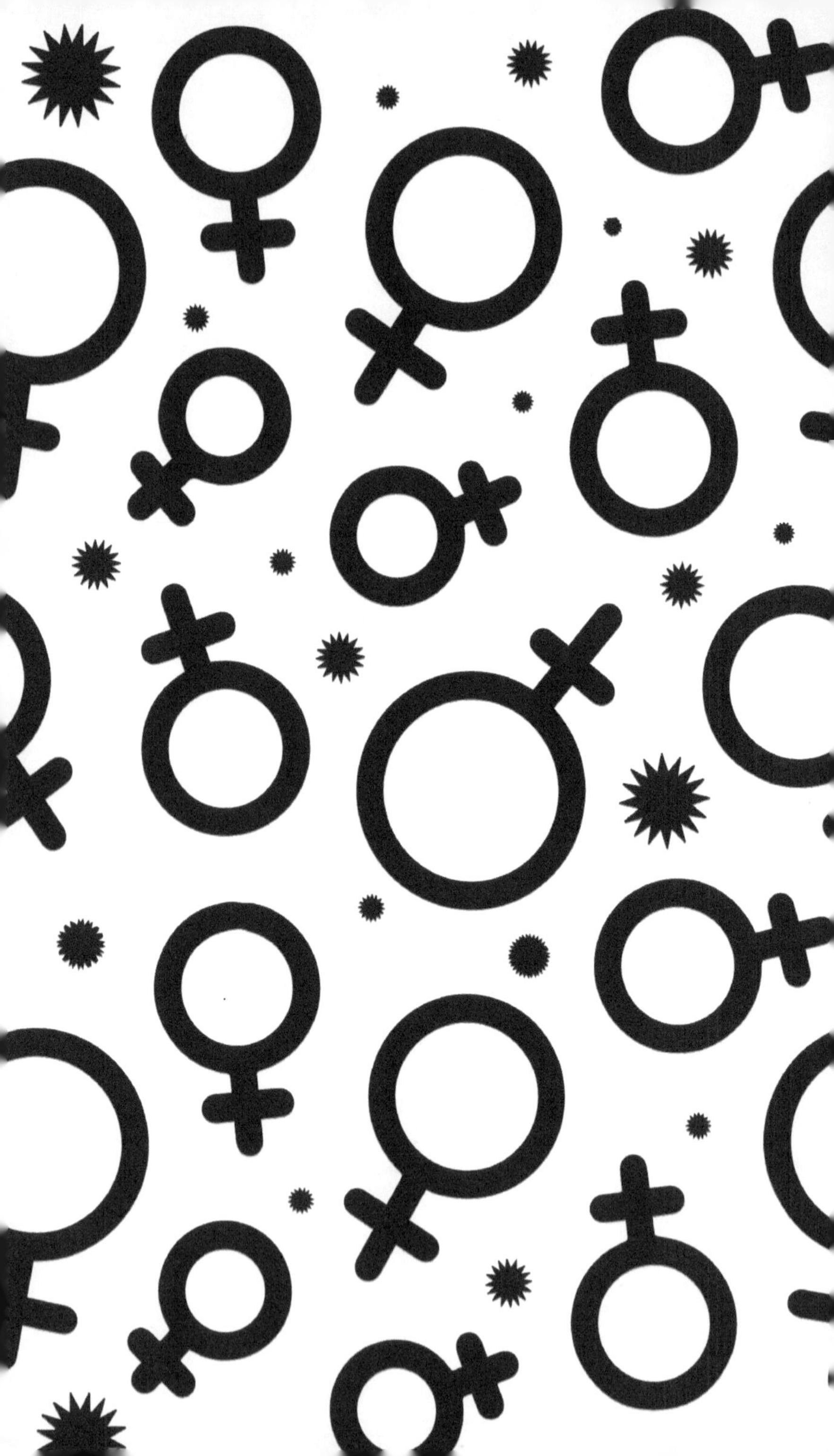

The Woman's Worth
Vicky Hamilton

I have always liked,
Being first and right.
But by just being a woman,
Sometimes makes me last and wrong,
No matter what the truth is.

Let me develop new talent,
But don't support me in my flight
       Fuck her hard enough,
And she will give up the plight.
Dive down just as the talent breaks,
No one will remember that it was her, not you,
Who put them in the race.

Am I really to pretty or emotional,
To manage the band?
Or is this what you tell yourself
So you can sleep at night?
You are just doing me a favor, right?
As it is a man who should finish the job.

A women's worth is mostly,
The love and care it takes to get them started.
Her words of love and wisdom makes them believe
The magic will happen.
She's the fire starter...the nurturing earth goddess,
However, in the music business,
It's the man's job to collect and eat all the bacon.

Cha-Ching, Bella Bing,
Wham Bam,
Thank you, Ma'am.

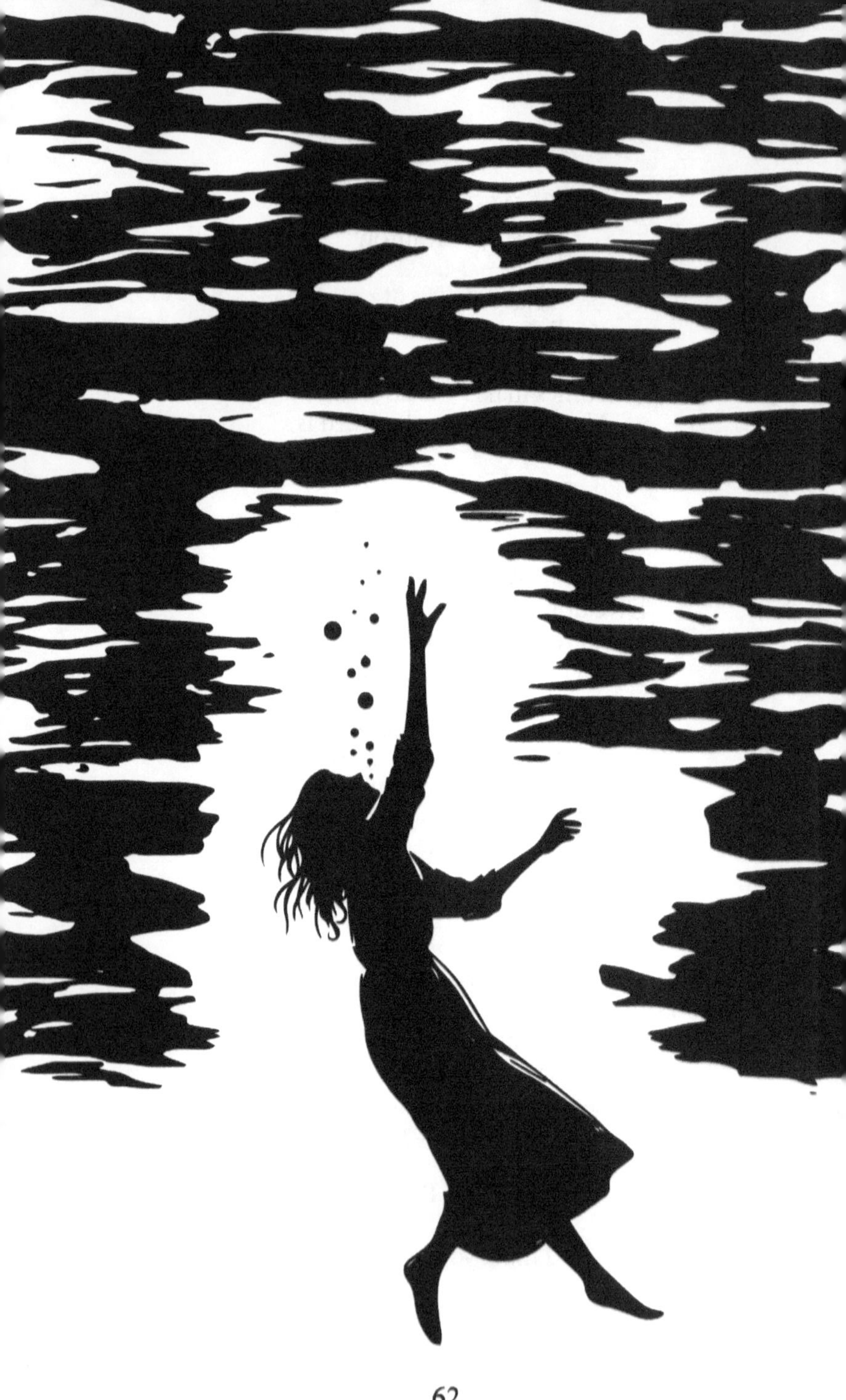

Broke and Broken
Vicky Hamilton

I am broke and broken.
I surrender.
Lift me up on wings of angels,
If I am to die of a broken heart.

I have finally,
Reached the bottom of my grief.
I am in acceptance,
That I could lose everything,
Including my life.

So God,
The last song is yours.
What song will you play?
As I swan song into the great unknown.

1981 - 2022

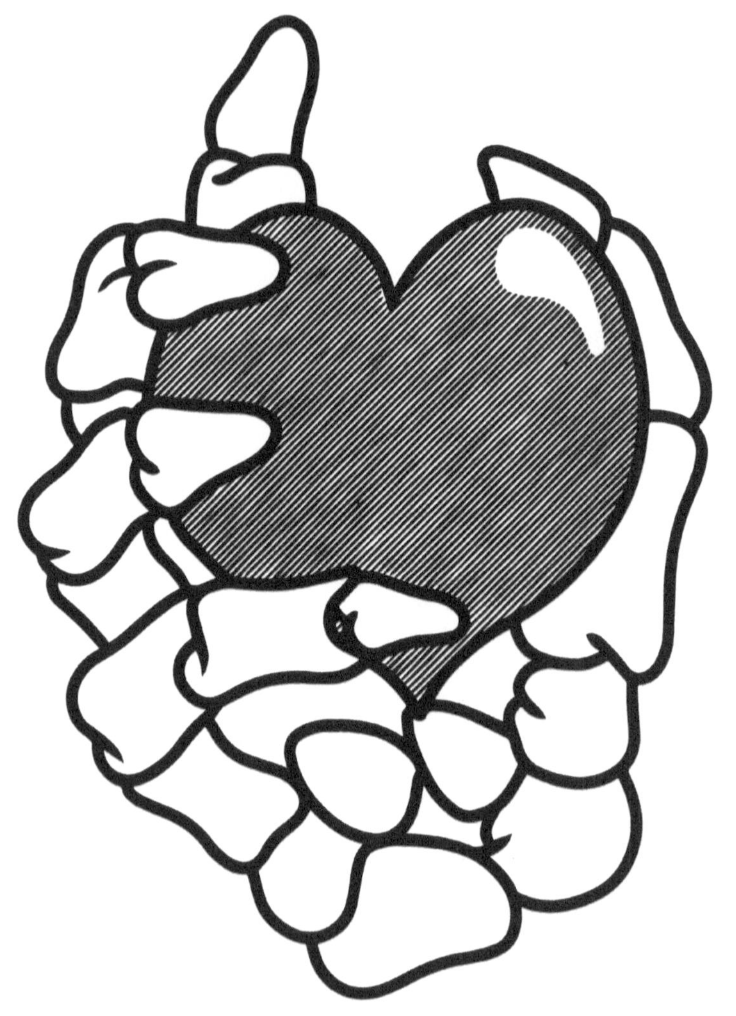

Pandemic
Vicky Hamilton

Has shut me in,
Locked you out.
Solitary confinement
Makes me yearn...*
To hear the roar of a crowd,
Taste freedom, dancing in the dark,
Or touch, the beat,
Of your heart.
The music holds the memory...*
Of all that is lost,
In the now forbidden fruit.

Mirrors
Vicky Hamilton

Beauty begets Beauty,
Lies create lies,
Fear breeds fear,
Faith elevates faith,
Passion initiates passion,
Pure thoughts receive pure thoughts,
Intimacy embraces intimacy,
Hate makes hate,
Trust equals trust,
Magic evolves magic,
Music repeats music,
Love builds love,
Truth mirrors truth.

2 LA
Vicky Hamilton

What is it about this town,
That sucks everyone in?
You come such a long way,
To get kicked in the teeth, again and again.

Is she really
The city of "Lost Angels"?
Poor souls, Renaissance heroes...
Searching for fame,
Perhaps to heal the pain,
From touching the flame,
In some past incarnation.

I sometimes think, she is the city,
Of lost Atlantis,
We've returned here to build the miracles,
We once knew....
Before we learnt about money and greed.

Or maybe it's a test of faith!
If we believe in miracles enough,
We will survive;
Earthquakes, riots, smog
And let's not forget,
The casting couch.

You must believe with all your might,
Because we know,
One glimmer of doubt,
Blows the candle out.

Why as a child,
Did I buy the illusion?
All that glistens is gold in Hollywood.
All songs sung with passion,
Revealed a true artist.

Only to find,
That the stars are as cold,
As the concrete they are imbedded in.

You must meet a lot of cretins,
To get to the cream.
Don't throw to much water,
On the flame,
Or all you 'll get is steam...
Hot steam.

I guess our favorite pussycat said it best,
"L.A. is like LegoLand,
Everything is plastic,
And when you least expect it,
It falls apart."

But what he forgot to say is ...,
We're always here,
To pick up the pieces,
Because,
We believe in miracles,
And
I believe in you,
If you believe in me,
All these lower flying demons can be beat.

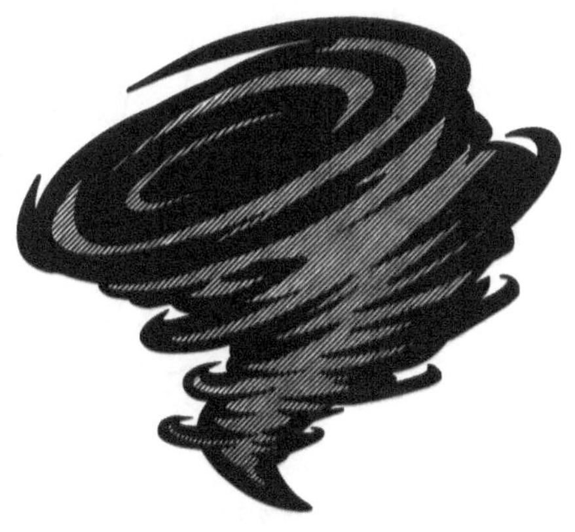

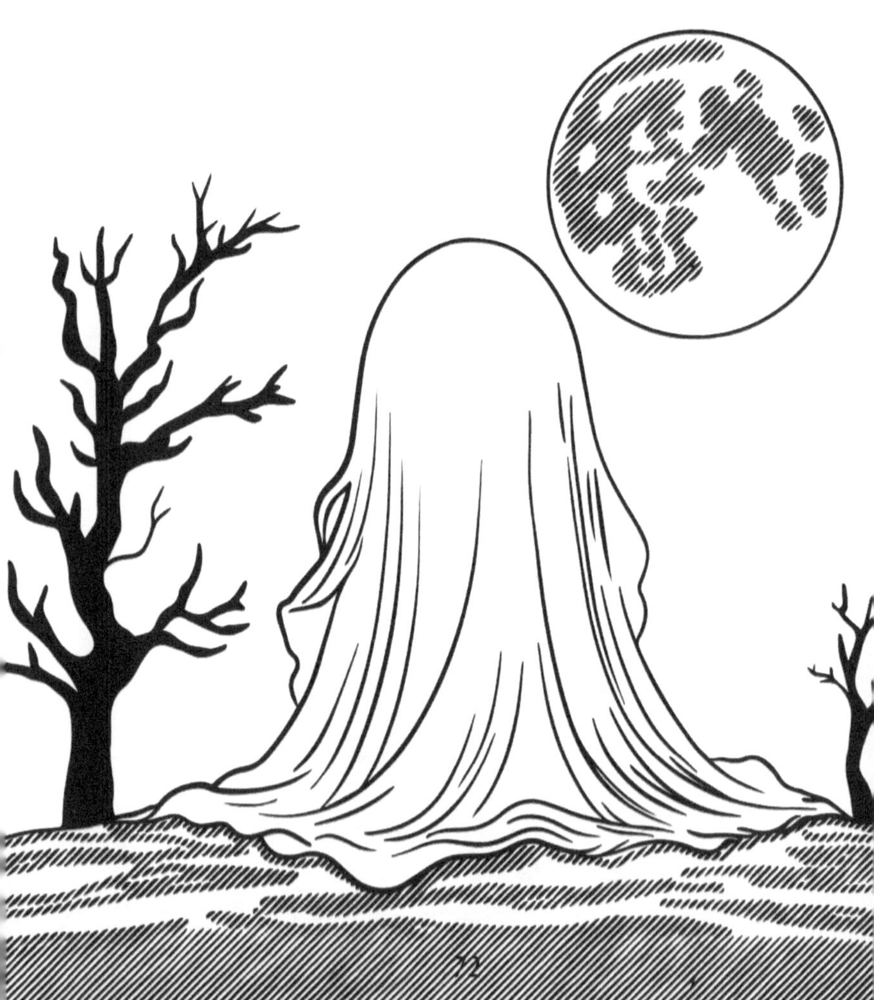

Your Ghost
Vicky Hamilton

The pumpkin full moon,
Rose over the mountain,
To smile that crooked smile

I heard your words,
Ring in my head,
Love like daylight always dies.

The ocean roared,
Behind my heels,
Like a angry lion in pain.

I turned around,
Quick enough,
To watch your ghost walk by,
In the rain.

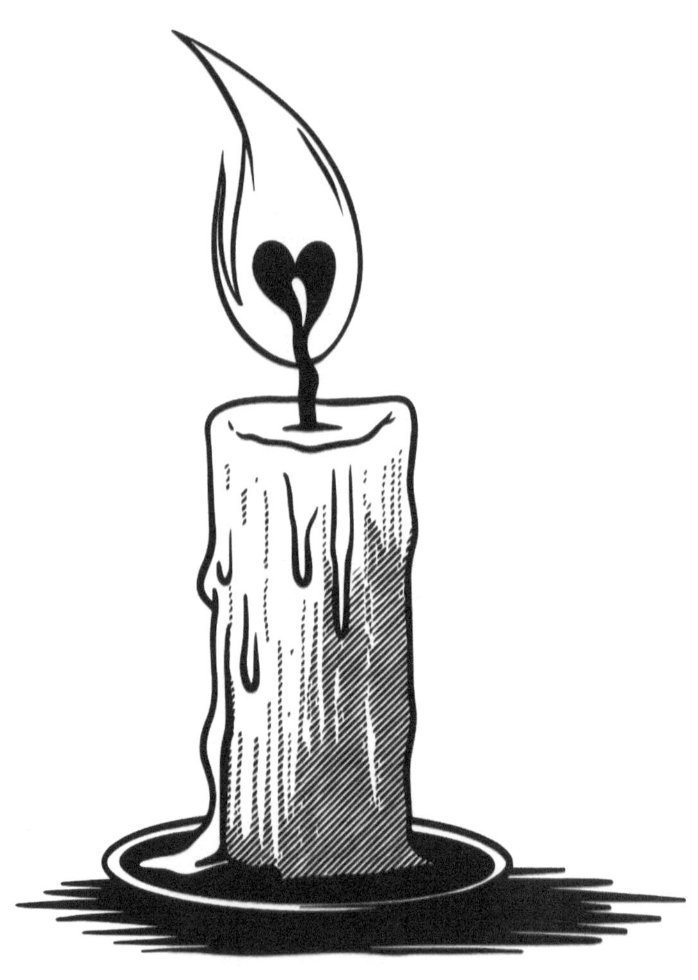

Affluent Archer
Vicky Hamilton

You pieced my heart from the backside,
Beautiful archer with a poison arrow,
I never saw it coming,
So blinded by love.

Sun goes down,
Like me, on my knees, for you.
Fireworks blaze in your eyes:
Crazy, faint, out of body, shape shifting heat.

The Halloween moon
Makes a second appearance
On a starry, starry Van Gogh night.
With a wish and a prayer,
The white candle I lit starts to flicker.

Our naked shadows intertwine on the wall
Bounce within the hot amorous ethers.
I loved you then, love you now, and foever after.
I close my eyes and wait your return,
If only in my dreams and memories.

Drink Me Up
Vicky Hamilton

I'm crawling back into my own skin.
Not the foreskin, of your little head,
Or
Your big head for that matter.

Yeah,
You are a piece of work...
Like that bitch in Key Largo.
You know all, don't you?
Except the meaning of Swan Song...
I guess this is the first time,
I can say to you,
Look it up, Nimrod.

Like the plastic swans bayside...
You couldn't shed a real tear.
Maybe now you'll lick it up.
Like you never would for me.

When your Mail Order Bride
Takes another American Prick,
With her subservient charm.
She'll have the last laugh...
And all your credit cards.

So ...
Happy New Year Sweet Tart.
You've got your freedom in your hands.
I hope she sparks your eternal fire.
If you can figure out what it is she really does.

Relationships that burn bright, like ours,
Illuminate darkness...
You really need to look at your words,
That didn't match your actions.

I really hope she breaks your heart,
The way you've broken mine.
While sipping your Bloody Mary,
You can drink to me.

That's right sweetheart,
Red Wine, like bloodletting,
Let me be your toast at midnight.
I'll be thinking of you.

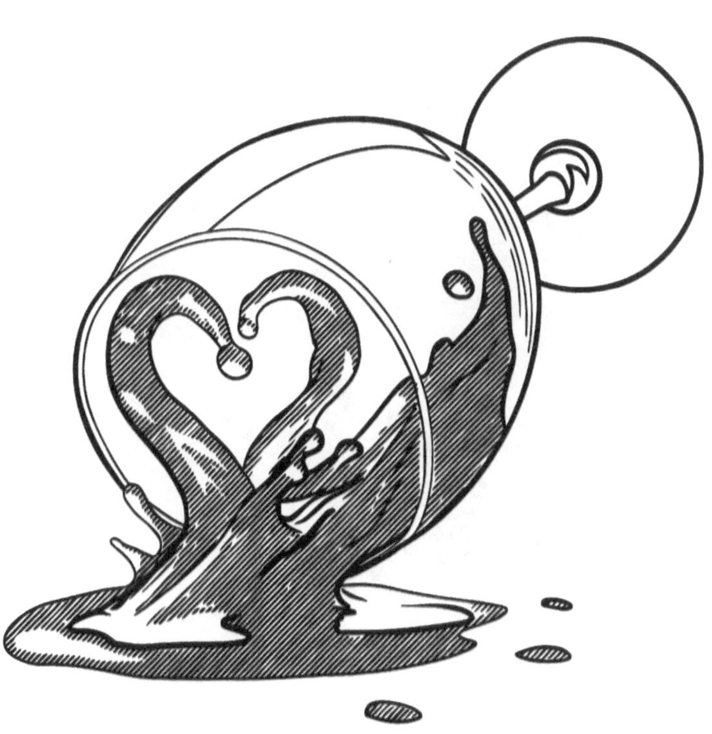

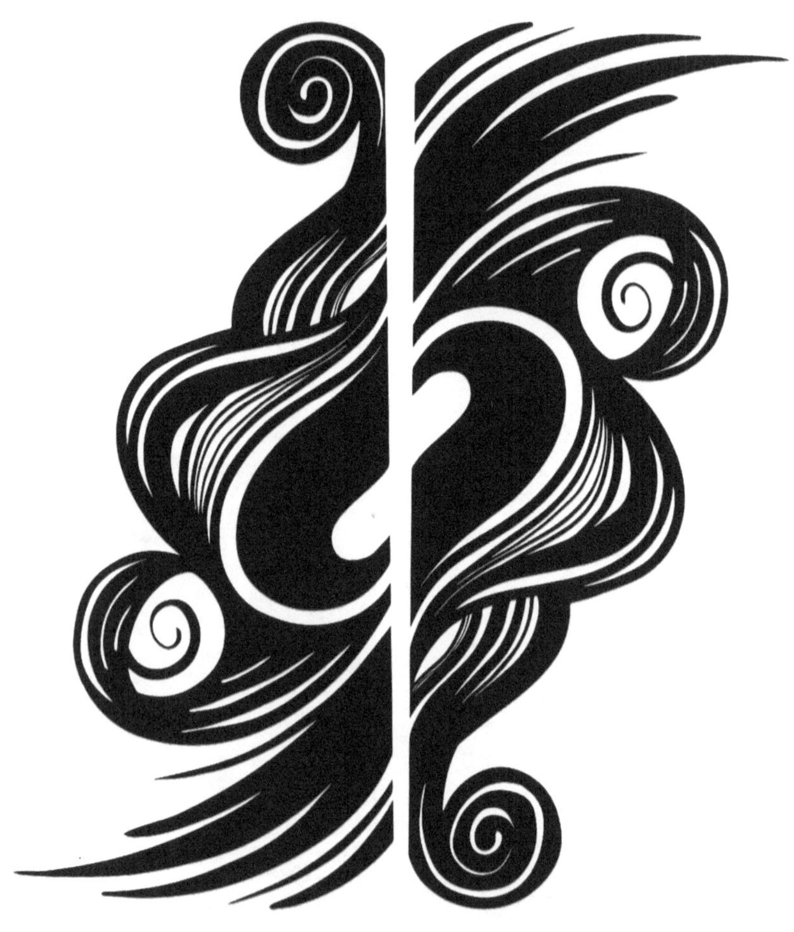

Searching for Clues
Vicky Hamilton

The only movie in town is,
Dead Again.
I guess that should have been my big clue.
Will I never escape you?
More the question,
Do I really want to escape you?

I guess the ying and yang were created for us.
It's a fine line,
Between your love,
And your hate.
I'd jump into the dark void,
If I could only find the gate.

Do you miss me?
I wonder if you'll miss me in the spring.
Will you remember the day,
I was your angel,
Also, your witch.
That changed your world.

Or will you my sweet,
Turn the other cheek?
Be careful what you wish for, my precious...
Spring always follows Winter...

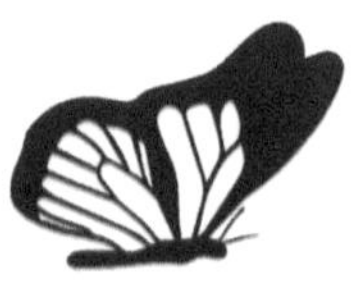

Totems
Vicky Hamilton

You are like the wild Spring,
Desert Flowers...
Beautiful and brilliant,
Colorful and free,
Blowing in the wind,
Still wild all the same.

I lay down in the meadow,
Thinking of you,
Kissing Butterflies...
As they flutter around my face.
The warm breeze upon me,
Whispers...
You are my forever friend.
Thank you.

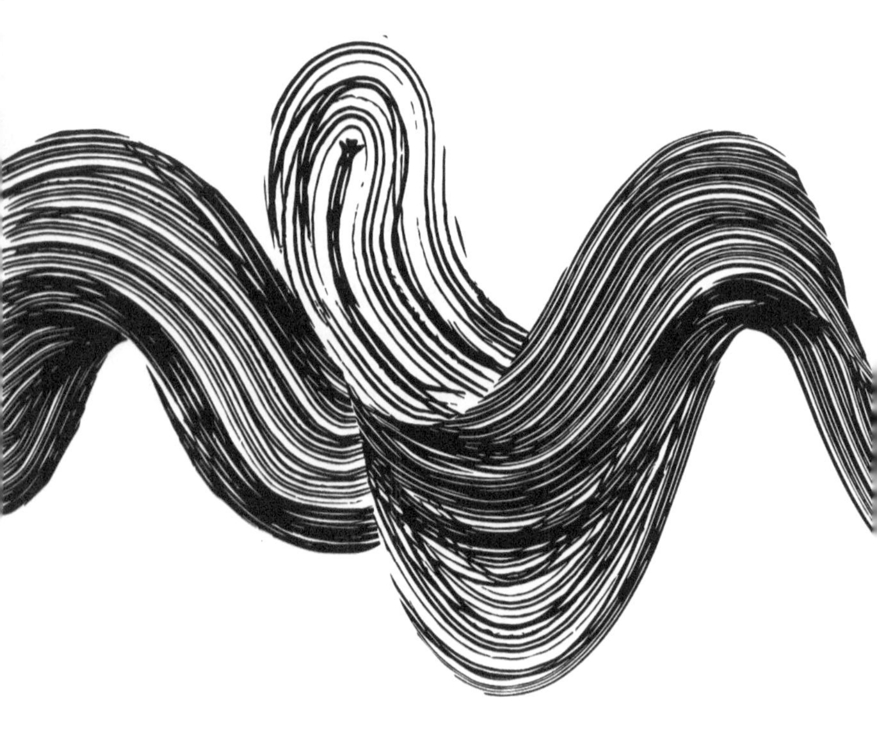

Silence
Vicky Hamilton

You call my voicemail and hang up!
Don't you have anything to say?
Or is it the tone of my voice,
You call to hear?

Do you miss your White Witch?
Do the things I said in earlier days,
Now ring true?

Do you miss my love?
The fusing of your muse.

Do you wish you could kiss me?
Or would a slap in the face,
Describe how you now feel.

I miss you.
It's true.
But your silence,
Feels like fear.

I live without you,
But I think of you daily.
We have such fiery potential...
The reality is,
You are too weak to speak.

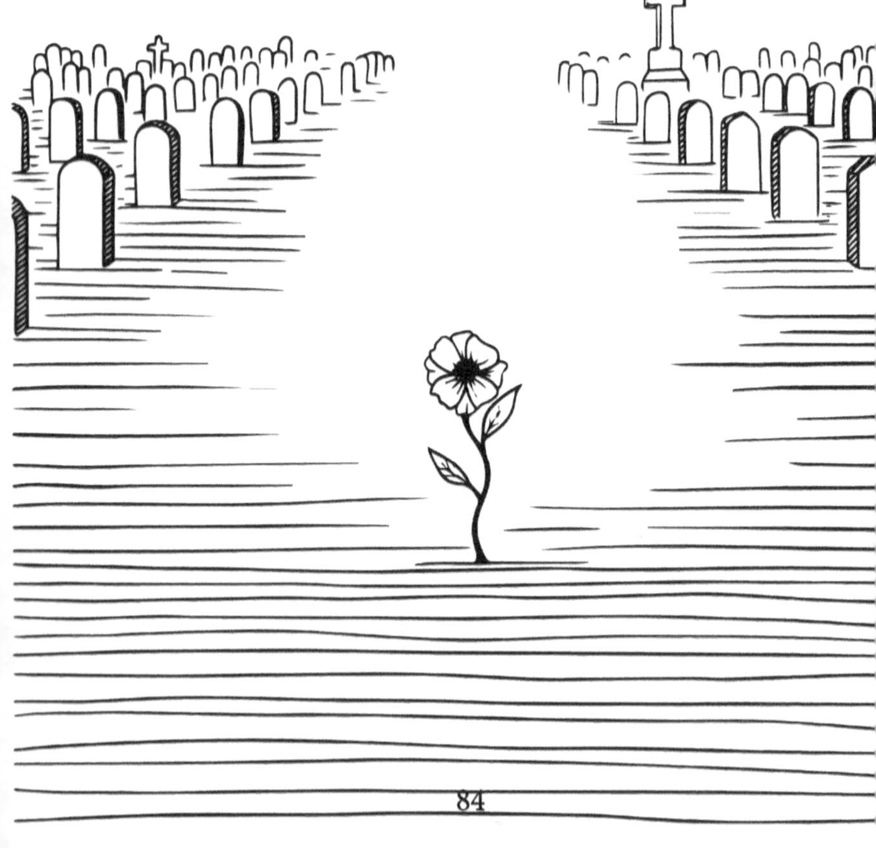

Pure
Vicky Hamilton

Love so pure,
So sobering,
Must be true.

Time,
Always precious,
Heart to heart.
A song about springtime,
The eternal now,
I don't want to waste a second.

Fuse my Muse
Vicky Hamilton

The happy house,
Isn't happy anymore.
I guess she knows I'm moving out.
Although it's the wind of change,
There is some hesitation and doubt.

A lot of good times,
Have come, have gone.
Then there was that long cold winter,
That instilled sadness,
On my heart.

For months I pondered,
What went wrong?
Was it...
Mortality, Past lives, Karma
Or just a change in present day songs?
Perhaps we weren't too honest with each other,
We spoke with our minds,
Instead of our hearts.
As Linda Goodman wrote of us;
"Some people love with restraint, as if they were some-
day to hate.
But we hated gently, carefully,
As if we were someday to love."

Maybe, this all happened,
Just so I could escape corporate greed.
It's true I feel like an angel,
Who's reclaimed her wings.
My hearts a little heavy,
My feathers a little beat up,
But my soul is excited,
My passion for art and music has regenerated here.

Still, when I dream,
I walk and talk with you.
I've come to one deep realization...
Out of all the flames in the world...
It's you,
Who fuses my muse.

So a clean slate hangs on the wall.
I'm glad we can begin again,
Whether or not we succeed, stumble or even fall,
I love you.
I miss you.
This is more than a want,
I need you
In my life,
To stand tall.

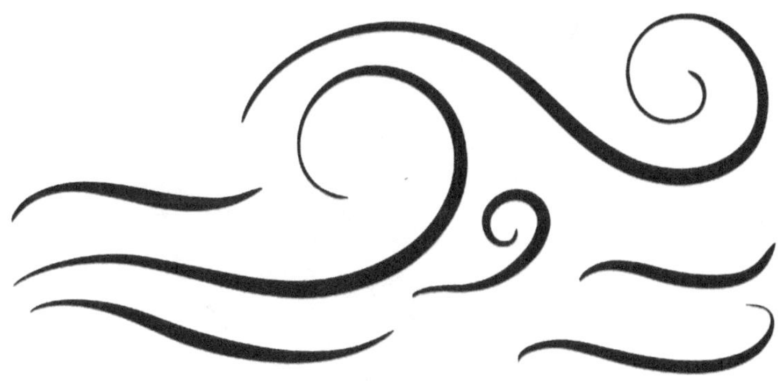

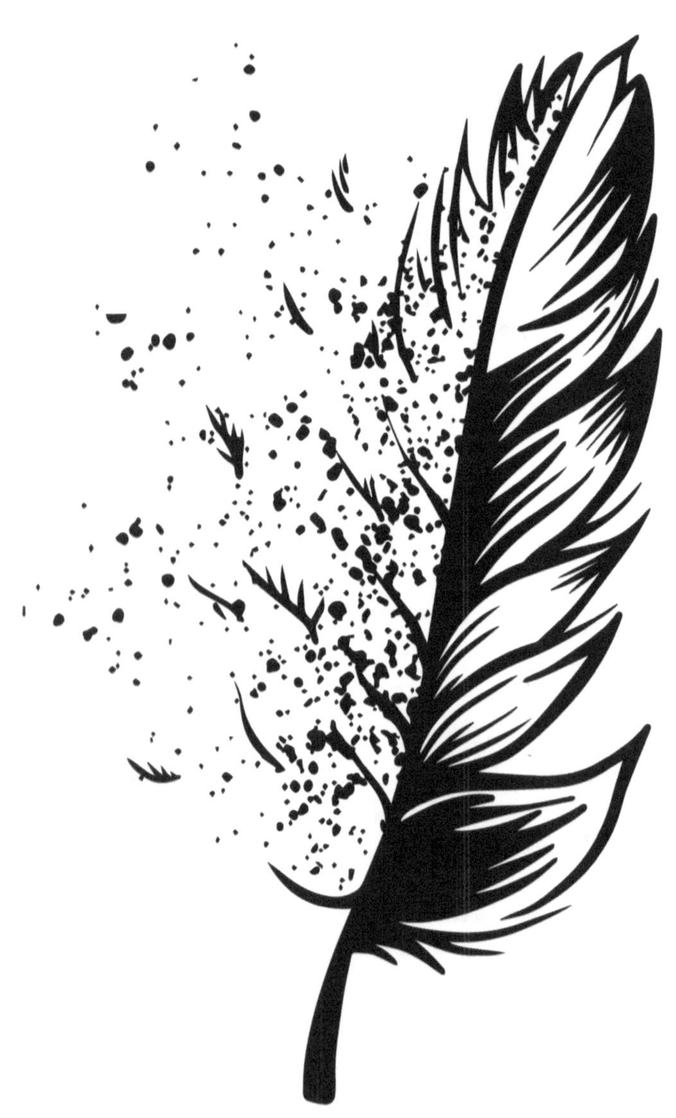

Goodbye
Vicky Hamilton

"I miss you,"
I said as I held your beautiful face,
In my hands.
The pain in your eyes,
Still shines.

"I unconditionally love you"
I whispered in your ear.
The truth can only be whispered.
"I'm trying to accept you for who you are,"
I cried,
But more importantly,
I am trying to accept you for who you are not.

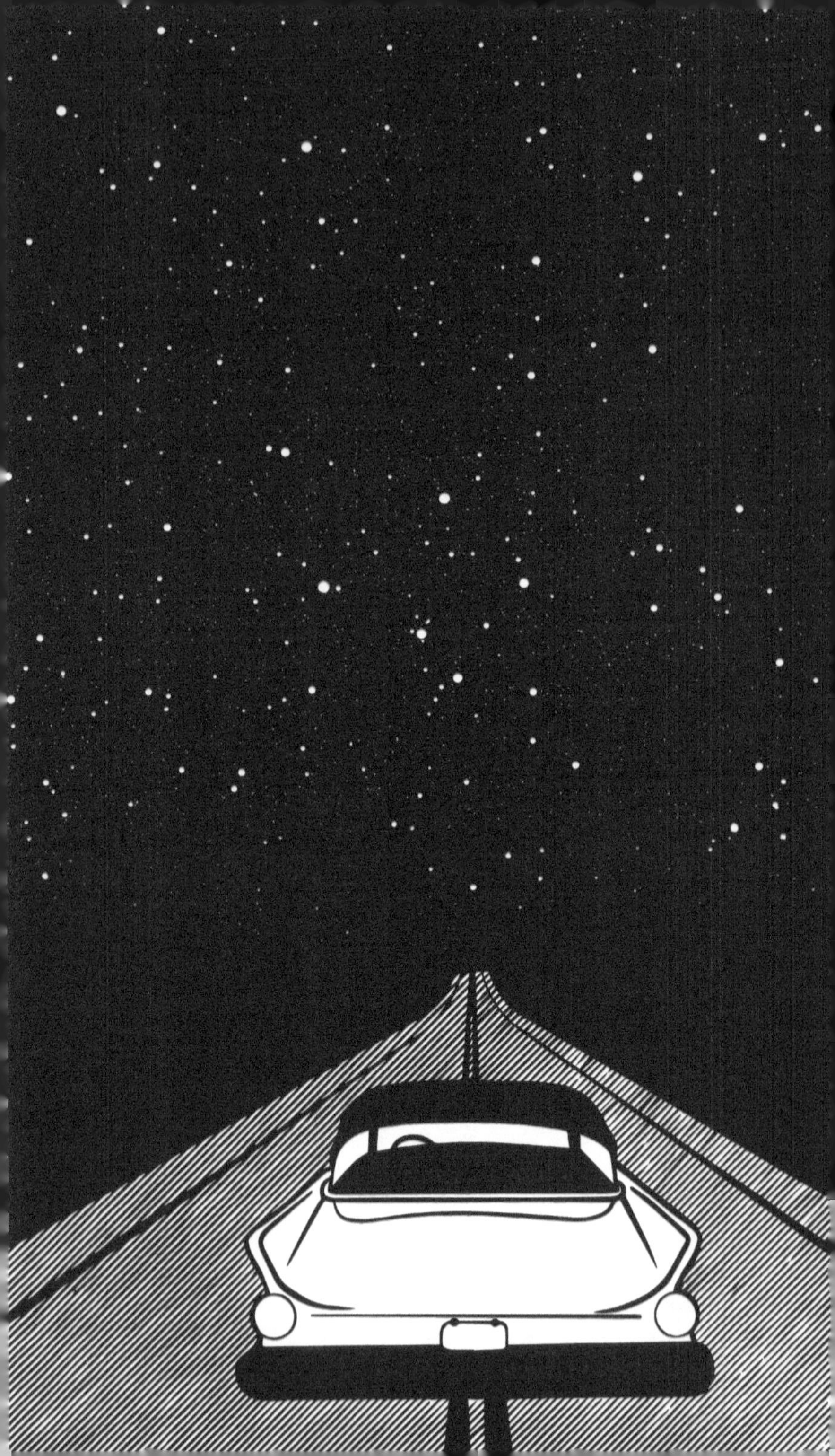

Everything's Over (Passion Crimes)

Music by Gregory Darling/ Darling Cruel /Polygram Records 1989

Tomorrow I will be gone,
I won't be hanging around,
Won't be your put down clown.

Tomorrow You are going to pay,
For all those things that you say,
You're love's a hateful thing.

(Chorus)
Everything's Over,
But the Shouting.
Everything's Over,
But the tears and goodbyes.
No lullabies.

You had it all in your mind,
You had it planned the whole time,
Little Dracula's bride.

But now the future's at hand
Won't go along with your plan,
I've had it up to here....

(2nd Chorus)

You put the gun to my head,
Strange ways, twisted fun.
You little slut on the run.
Tomorrow I will be gone,
Before the break of dawn,
I'll be singing my song.

(3rd Chorus)

No Alibis

Star Collector

Music by Gregory Darling/ Darling Cruel /Polygram Records 1989

Star Collector had immortal dreams,
Danced his way on to every scene,
He don't care,
He's for real.

He's a red top spinning around
The music show.
Where he goes, nobody knows...
He's too shy, He's so high,
He flies into the darkest night.

(Chorus)
Hang around in town,
Dreaming of a sound.
The days of rain and pain,
You better shop around.
The Star Collector's sound.

There is a ghost in your closet,
And a bitch in your bed.
Last nights memories,
Make you wish you were dead.
It's so cold, It's so cold.

Watch out boy,
There's a man on your back.
Taking all your dreams,
Throws them all away.
He don't care,
It's not fair.
Your home is not your own.

(2nd Chorus)
Star Collector,
Don't you know, you are on your own.
Your only best friend is yourself.
Get off the stage,
There is a price to be paid,
For those of us,
Who have to suffer in vain.
Dream on, rock cowboy.
Dream until your dream comes true.

Star Collector
Wrote a book on life.
Cashed in his dreams,
Has a beautiful wife.
A white house, a big car,
A mink guitar.
Now he's a big big star.

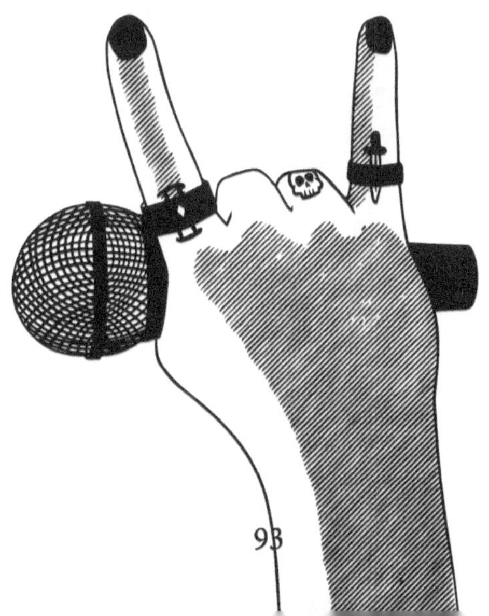

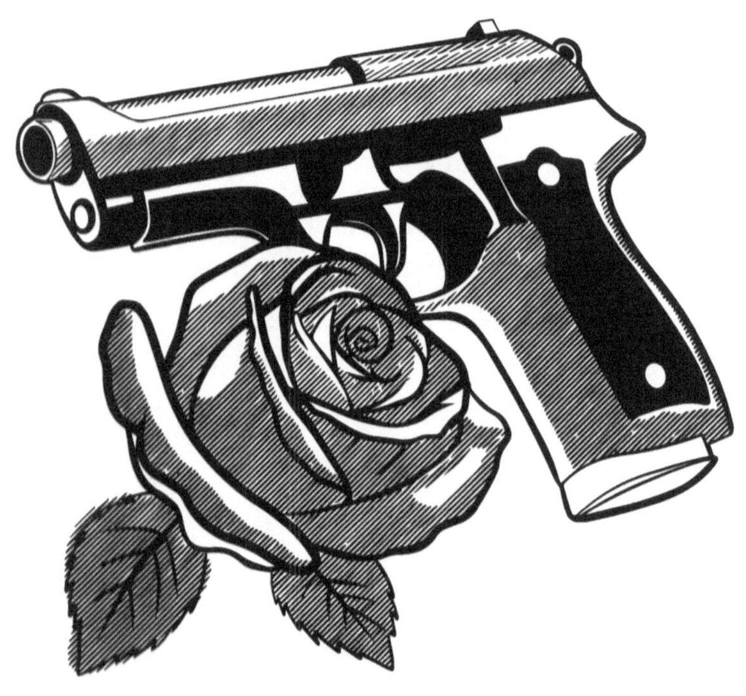

Tales of Emotions
Vicky Hamilton

Music by Gregory Darling/ Darling Cruel /Polygram Records 1989

Josephine and Mr. Blvd.
Built a castle in the valley of dolls.
Let's get to moving,
In your American car.
Down the highway,
Where the moon meets the stars.

(Chorus)
Tales of emotion,
Forbidden devotion.
Tales of emotion,
Forbidden devotion.
Power and Passion,
The oldest of fashion.

In Love Obsession,
There is no key to protection.
Love your Mother,
But don't love your lover.
In love injection,
There is no fear of rejection
Josephine I think I discovered.

(2nd and 3rd Chorus)
Tales of emotion
It's better to have lost
And have loved.
It's better to love,
Than to be loved.

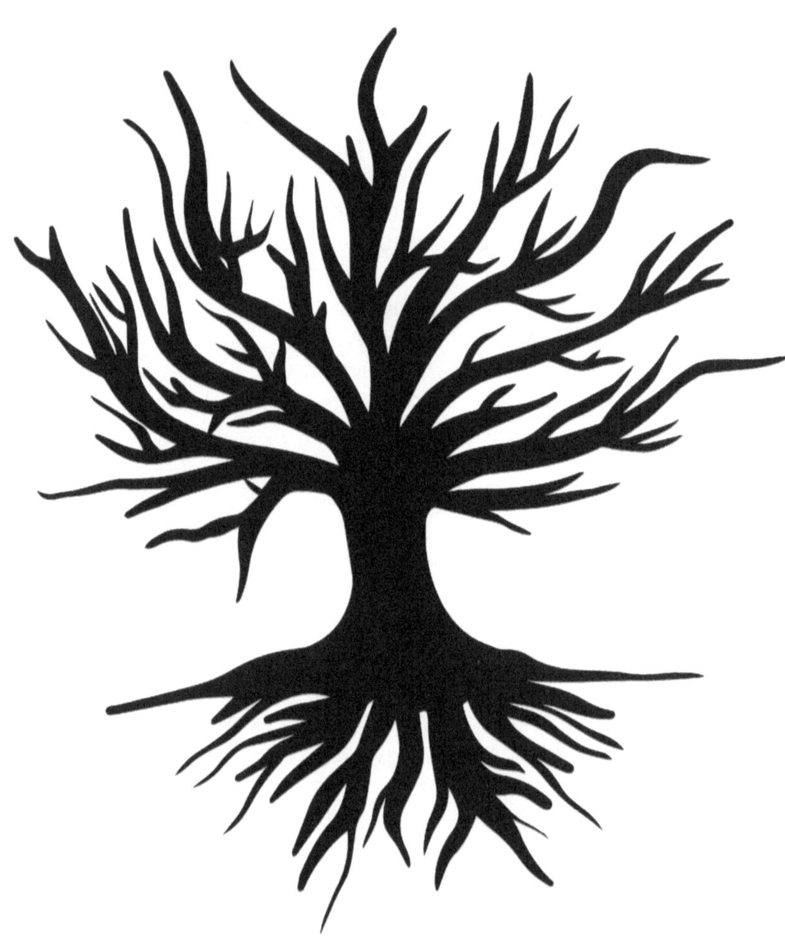

The Pure Heart of my Mother's Love
Vicky Hamilton

Dear Mother,
You have taught me so much.
Though,
The things I remember most,
Revolve around love.

Looking back,
On all the years.
When you supported me,
And
Wiped away my tears.
When I fell down,
Your encouraging words,
Gave me strength,
To get back up...
Then start over again.

Perhaps,
Your biggest show of love,
Is your selfless devotion,
To this family.

When I moved to L.A.
You hugged me,
Cried tears of love...
You gave me my wings,
While praying to Guardian Angels above.

I love you Mom.
Probably more than you will ever know.
I thank the Lord each day,
For such a beautiful beginning.
That gives me faith and courage,
To follow my dreams.

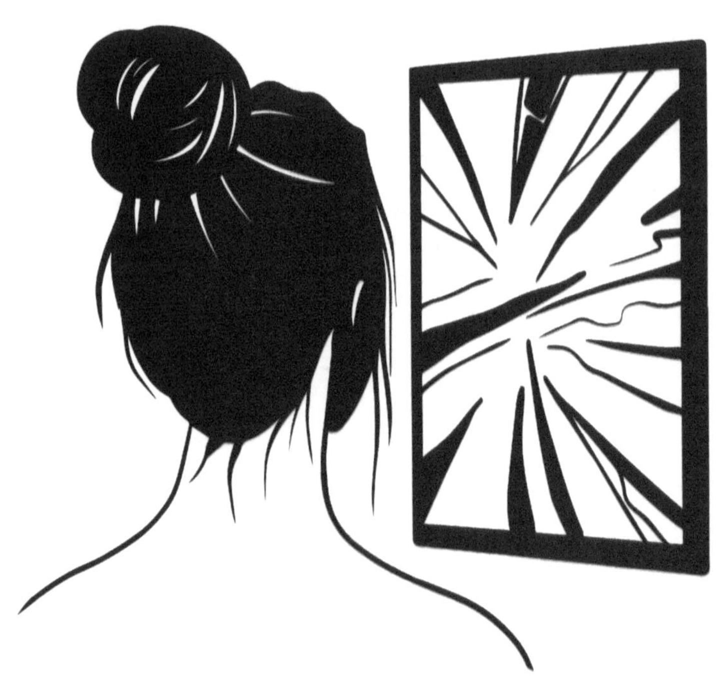

In Anger
Vicky Hamilton

She loves to masturbate,
Always taking the easy way...
Out of her body,
Out of her mind...
Maybe this time,
She'll escape him forever.

Back to Earth...
His words, ring in her head.
This love he makes her feel...
Makes her wish,
She was dead.

She called herself,
Mary Magdalene.
She says she showed Jesus a good time,
Without guilt for sin.
She looks to her higher self,
To be saved from the madness.
God made her a woman,
For the boys club to bleed on.

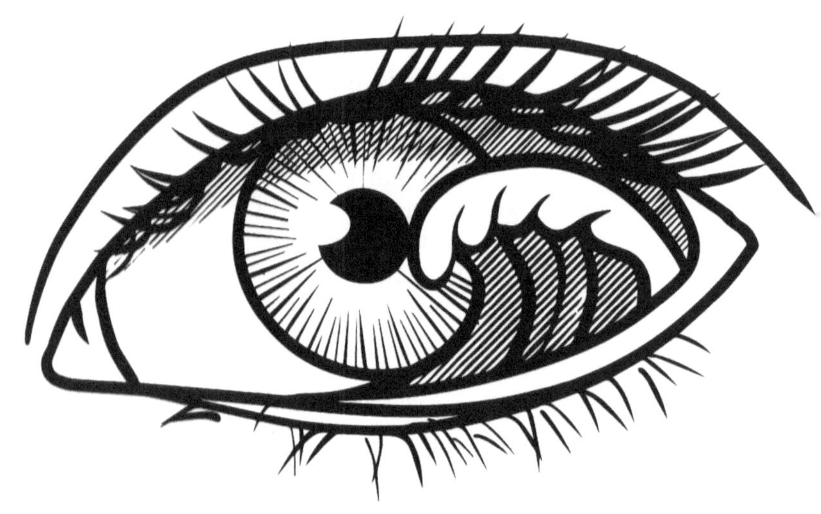

Let Me Be Your Ocean
Vicky Hamilton

Let me be your ocean,
Deep and blue.
Let me be your serenity,
Calm, clear and true.

I see you in my heart,
When I look into your eyes.
I can never find the words...
You always run, always hide.

I guess I'm just a coward,
I'm afraid to hear,
What you might feel.
It's easier to embrace the yearning,
Than to know,
It could never be.

So let me be your ocean.
Always wanting,
Always churning.
Let my love be your lighthouse,
Always bright,
Always true,
Always home.

If one night,
You come to call,
I'll know God has heard my prayers.
I pray to be your island,
The heartland of your dreams.

1974 - 1981

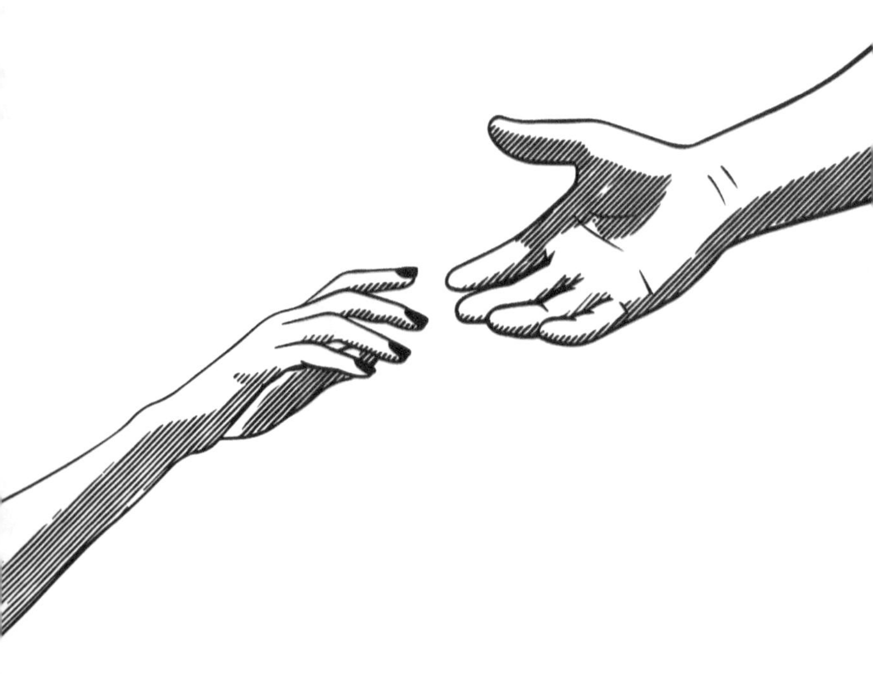

Meaning
Vicky Hamilton

Being with you has lots of meaning,
You give me a wonderful feeling.
I know I play around too much,
Maybe it's because I like your touch?
People may say we're not right,
But we will just have to fight!
Give me your hand and walk the land,
Together...
We'll make a stand.

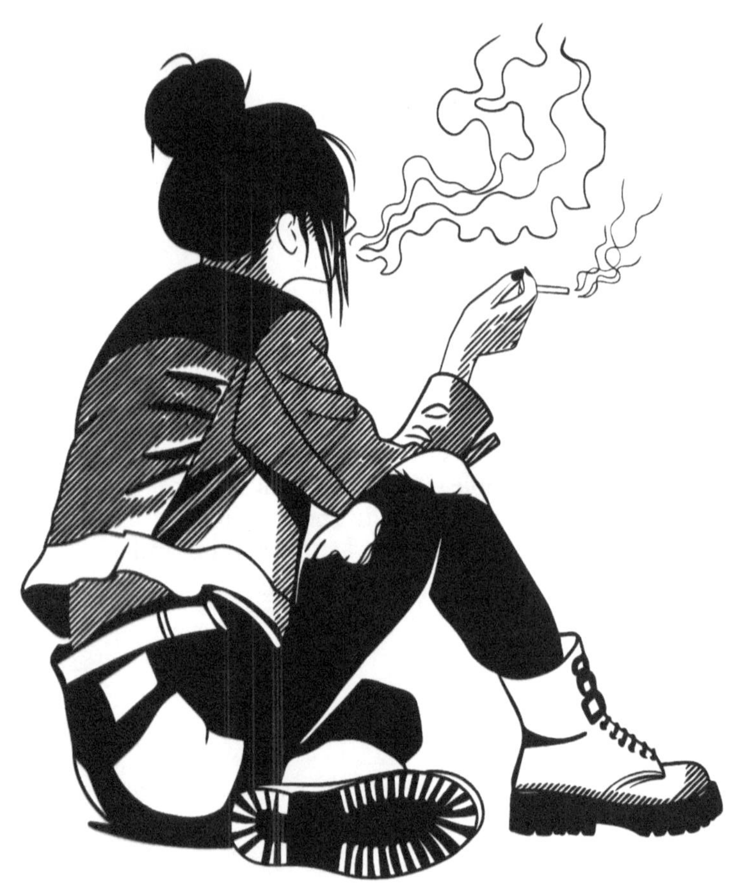

Clouds
Vicky Hamilton

Why do clouds turn black?
Why do teens all wear blue jean slacks?
Why do flames always die?
Why do good things always end?
Just when my love for you began.

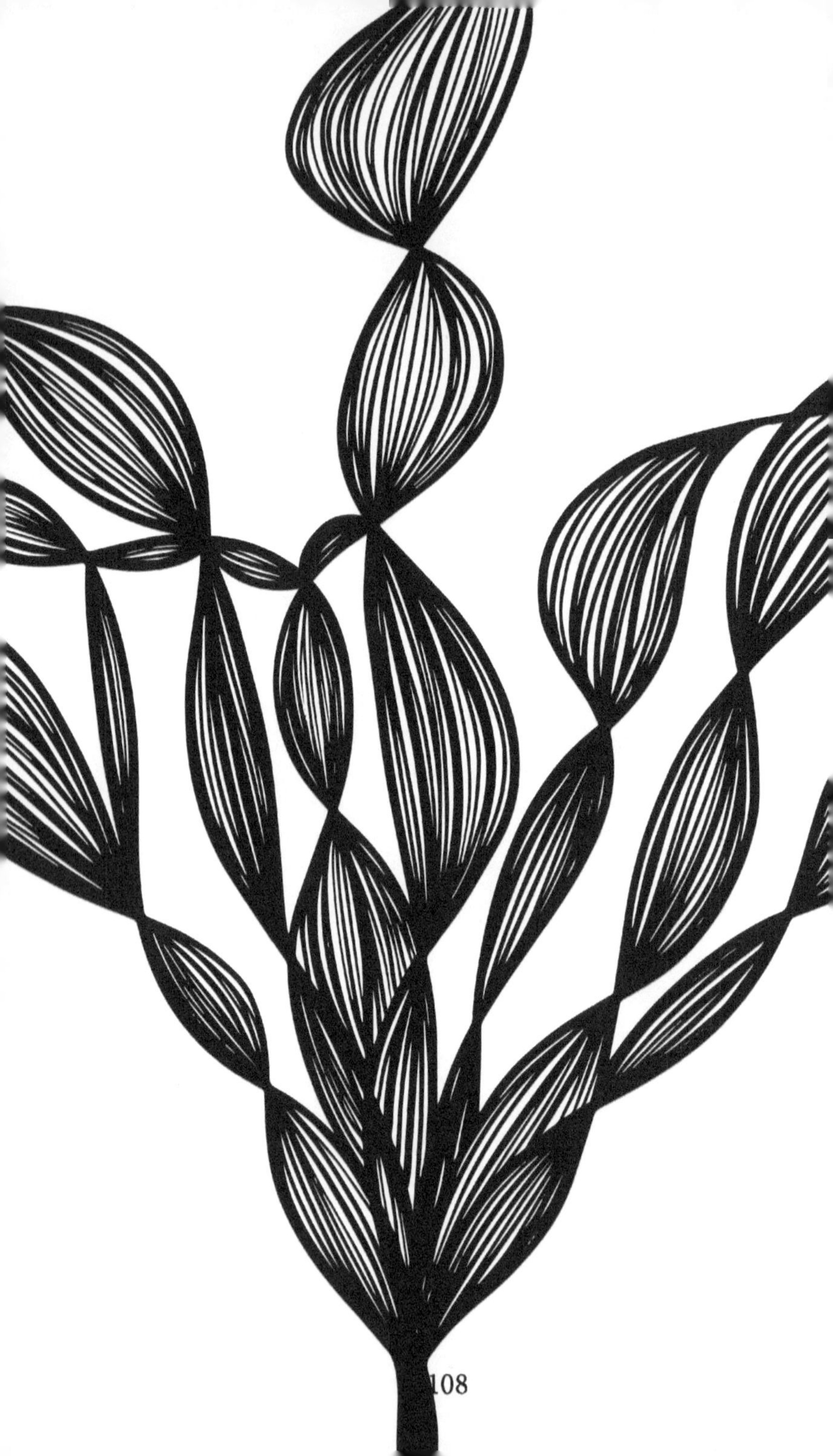

Mr. Natural
Vicky Hamilton

Colors of time keep flying by,
Sometimes you think you'd rather die.
How can you tell a bad trip from the good?
You can't, there is no way you possibly could.
Fun times, fly fast...
Years from now where will we be?
My God,
Don't let my friends leave me.
We can chase the stars,
Not sure which way we will go...
Because to you, Mr. Natural,
I can never say no!

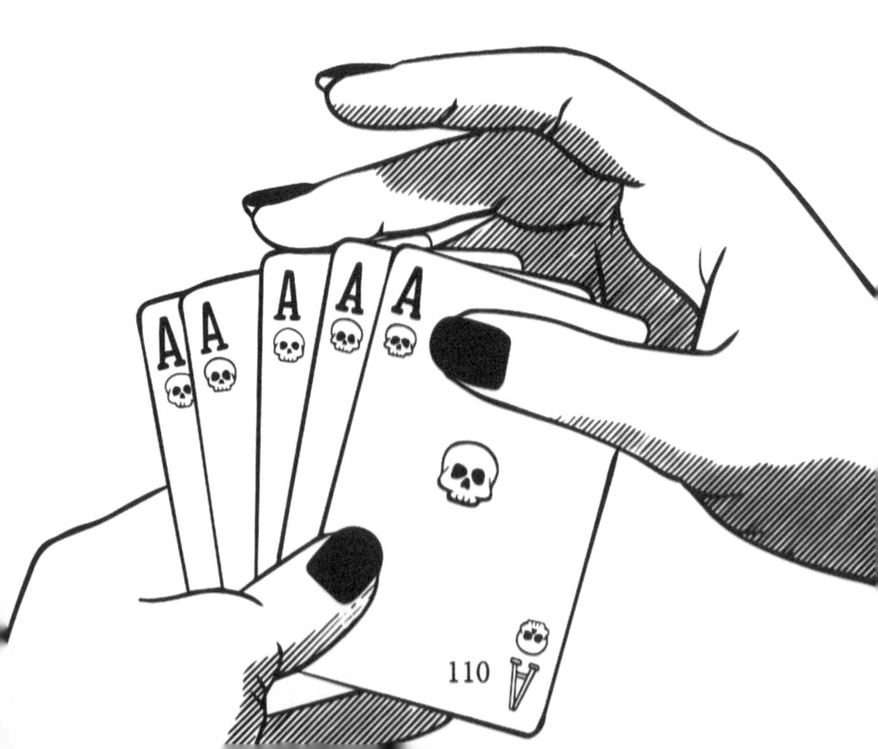
A
A
A
A
A
110

Time
Vicky Hamilton

Troubled times all around,
They put you under and knock you down.
Don't worry about me,
I'll get it together,
You'll see.

I exist only in myself,
Many times, I have dealt,
The wrong cards...
But you'll see,
I'll remove these scars.

So, live for today,
Don't worry over tomorrow...
Good things are to come,
There's so much time to borrow.

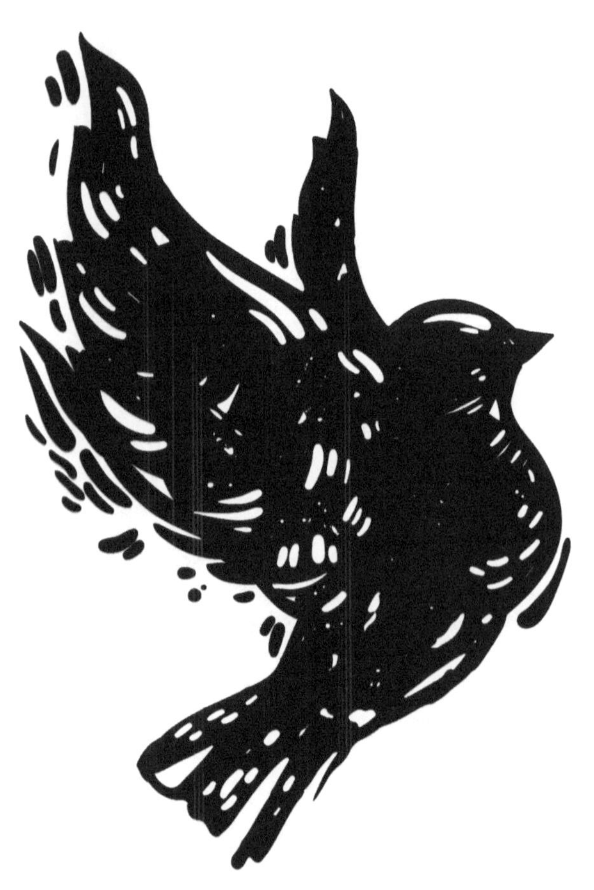

Peace
Vicky Hamilton

P is for the **Privilege** of loving you
And being loved.
E is for the **Ease** it gives the
Soul and Mind...
A is for the **Answers** in your Search to
Find yourself...
C is the **Calm** you feel if you like
What you find....
E is for **Everlasting....**

May this love never cease,
PEACE

About the Author
Vicky Hamilton

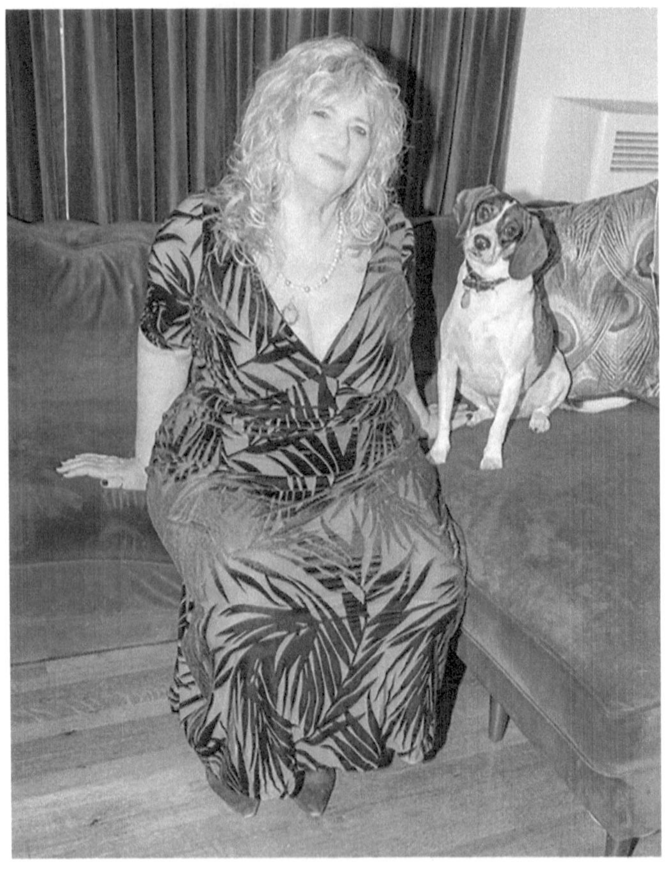

Vicky & Pluto
Photo by Liz

Long time Grammy Award-Winning music industry executive, personal manager and writer. Vicky is featured in; I Wanna Rock docuseries, and June documentary, both released on Paramount Plus, VH-1's Behind the Music and Driven, The BBC, The Biography Channel and many other music documentaries.

Considered one of the most successful female executives in the music industry, Vicky has discovered, developed or managed the careers of Guns N' Roses, Motley Crue, Poison, Faster Pussycat and many others. Sales figures of the acts Vicky has developed are over 250 million records in sales.

In addition, Vicky Hamilton also has worked as an A&R executive at Geffen, Capitol and Vapor Records and had a successful independent record label, which won a Grammy for June Carter Cash's, Press On record.

Currently, Vicky has finished a worldwide book tour for her memoir, Appetite For Dysfunction recorded the book as an audio book that was released 2023 on Arena Scripts. Appetite for Dysfunction is now being developed as TV series by production company Electric Panda.

As always, Vicky is managing and consulting several music acts, owns her own record label, Dark Spark Music distributed through The Orchard/Sony.

For more info, visit:

www.vickyhamilton.com
www.darksparkmusic.com